CAMPAIGN 395

THE WINTER CAMPAIGN IN ITALY 1943

Orsogna, San Pietro and Ortona

PIER PAOLO BATTISTELLI ILLUSTRATED BY JOHNNY SHUMATE

Series editor Nikolai Bogdanovic

OSPREY PUBLISHING
Bloomsbury Publishing Plc
Kemp House, Chawley Park, Cumnor Hill, Oxford OX2 9PH, UK
29 Earlsfort Terrace, Dublin 2, Ireland
1385 Broadway, 5th Floor, New York, NY 10018, USA
E-mail: info@ospreypublishing.com
www.ospreypublishing.com

OSPREY is a trademark of Osprey Publishing Ltd

First published in Great Britain in 2023

A catalogue record for this book is available from the British Library.

ISBN: PB 9781472855695; eBook 9781472855701; ePDF 9781472855718; XML 9781472855688

23 24 25 26 27   10 9 8 7 6 5 4 3 2 1

Maps by Bounford.com
3D BEVs by Paul Kime
Index by Mark Swift
Typeset by PDQ Digital Media Solutions, Bungay, UK
Printed and bound in India by Replika Press Private Ltd.

Osprey Publishing supports the Woodland Trust, the UK's leading woodland conservation charity.

MIX
Paper from responsible sources
FSC® C016779
www.fsc.org

Artist's note

Readers can discover more about the work of illustrator Johnny Shumate at the below website:
https://johnnyshumate.com

To find out more about our authors and books visit **www.ospreypublishing.com**. Here you will find extracts, author interviews, details of forthcoming events and the option to sign up for our newsletter.

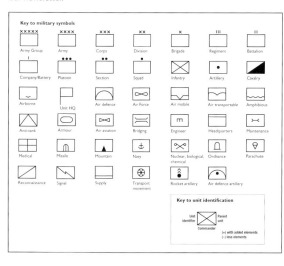

Author's acknowledgements

The author gratefully acknowledges the help and support provided by Marc Romanych of the Digital History Archive, Robert Forczyk, Dave Kerr, the Museo della Battaglia di Ortona, Dieter Nell of the Bund Deutscher Fallschirmjäger e.V., Lt.Col. (ret.) Dr Christopher Pugsley (Wakanae, New Zealand), Dr Klaus Schmider (Sandhurst), and last but not least the series editor Nikolai Bogdanovic, whose help and support proved invaluable.

Author's dedication

In memory of my parents, Angelo ('Lillo') Battistelli and Alliata Vera.

Unit designations

Allied units are denoted by their abbreviated nationality (e.g. BR, US, CDN, etc.). German units retain their original-language denominations, as per Armee Oberkommando (AOK, army), Korps (corps – Armee, Panzer, Fallschirm, Gebirgs or generic, armoured, parachute and mountain), and Division – Infanterie (infantry, subsequently redesignated Grenadier), Panzer (armoured), Panzergrenadier (mechanized infantry), Fallschirmjäger (paratroop), Gebirgs (mountain) and Jäger (light infantry). Italian units (now fighting for the Allies) also retain their original language denominations: Reggimento (regiment), Battaglione (battalion) – Motorizzato (motorized), Fanteria (infantry).

Battalions of regiments are referred to using Roman numerals, e.g. I./363rd RCT (1st Battalion, 363rd Regimental Combat Team), or I./FJR 1 (I.Bataillon, Fallschirmjäger-Regiment 1). Companies within regiments are referred to using Arabic numerals or letters, e.g. A./I./363rd RCT (Company A, 1st Battalion, 363rd Regimental Combat Team).

Abbreviations and acronyms

AFV	armoured fighting vehicle
AOK	Armee Oberkommando
BR	British (United Kingdom)
CDN	Canadian
FJR	Fallschirmjäger-Regiment
FR	French
GR	Grenadier-Regiment
HGr	Heeresgruppe (army group)
HQ	Headquarters
IND	Indian
KGr	Kampfgruppe (battle group)
mot.	motorisiert
NZ	New Zealander
PAK	Panzer Abwehr Kanone (anti-tank gun)
PGR	Panzergrenadier-Regiment
PIAT	Projector Infantry Anti-Tank
PIR	Parachute Infantry Regiment
QF	quick-firing
RCT	Regimental Combat Team
SSF	Special Service Force
US	United States

Canadian regimental abbreviations

CYR	Carleton and York Regiment
HOC	Highlanders of Canada
HPER	Hastings and Prince Edward Regiment
LER	Loyal Edmonton Regiment
PLDG	Princess Louise Dragoon Guards
PPCLI	Princess Patricia's Canadian Light Infantry
QRR	Queen's Royal Regiment
R22e	Royal 22e Régiment
RCR	Royal Canadian Regiment
SHC	Seaforth Highlanders of Canada
TRR	Three Rivers Regiment
WNSR	West Nova Scotia Regiment

Front cover main illustration: Canadian infantry, protected by armour, fight their way into the centre of the town of Ortona, December 1943. (Johnny Shumate)

Title page photograph: A Canadian gunner from the Loyal Edmonton Regiment Anti-Tank Battery fires a 6-pdr QF anti-tank gun against German positions in Ortona on 21 December 1943. (Photo by Terry F. Rowe/Keystone/Hulton Archive/Getty Images)

CONTENTS

The Italian front, September 1943–January 1944

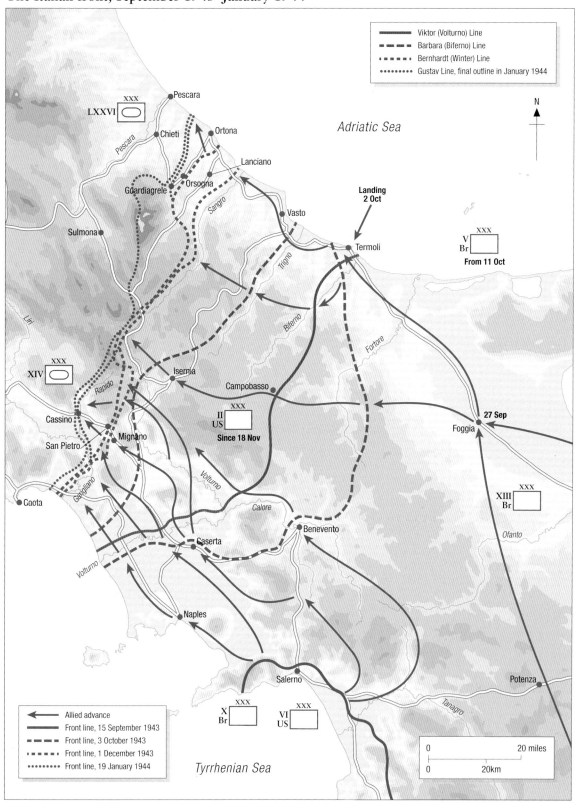

Viktor (Volturno) Line
Barbara (Biferno) Line
Bernhardt (Winter) Line
Gustav Line, final outline in January 1944

N

Adriatic Sea

LXXVI XXX

Pescara
Pescara
Chieti
Ortona
Lanciano
Orsogna
Guardiagrele
Sangro
Vasto
Landing 2 Oct
Sulmona
Trigno
Termoli
V Br XXX
From 11 Oct

Biferno

XIV XXX

Liri
Isernia
Campobasso
Fortore
Rapido
II US XXX
Since 18 Nov
Cassino
Mignano
San Pietro
27 Sep
Foggia
Volturno
Calore
XIII Br XXX
Gaeta
Garigliano
Ofanto
Benevento
Caserta
Volturno
Naples
Potenza
Tanagro
Salerno

Allied advance
Front line, 15 September 1943
Front line, 3 October 1943
Front line, 1 December 1943
Front line, 19 January 1944

X Br XXX
VI US XXX

Tyrrhenian Sea

0   20 miles
0   20km

ORIGINS OF THE CAMPAIGN

In late October 1943, the Allied Chiefs of Staff still believed that their forces 'could be in Rome before Christmas'. Such an illusory opinion is revealing of the attitude with which both sides approached the Italian campaign. From the Allied side, before US Fifth Army's landing at Salerno and the British seizure of Taranto, coupled with BR Eighth Army's advance in Calabria, no one had a clear idea of what to do next. The only certainty was Rome, the ideal goal of the entire campaign.

By 17 September, as the Germans withdrew from Salerno and BR Eighth Army made its way up Italy's boot, the Allied commanders were convinced that German forces would withdraw to northern Italy. Thus, tying down German units and preventing their possible use in North-West Europe became the immediate aim of Allied strategy. That Hitler considered this option as well is revealing of the complete uncertainty surrounding the early stages of the campaign.

Concerned by an Allied move against the Balkans, Hitler took into account the defence of southern Italy only insofar as it could help by reacting to a landing in Greece or Yugoslavia. The only other reason for maintaining control of most of the country was exploitation. As such, the Italian campaign assumed its final form in an almost accidental manner. While Hitler ordered a slow withdrawal from southern Italy in order to gain time, generals Dwight D. Eisenhower and Harold Alexander planned a two-pronged drive on Rome by means of an amphibious landing just south of the city.

In October 1943, the plan seemed feasible. The Allied armies began advancing up the Italian peninsula, slowly but successfully. The first German lines of defence were crushed, thanks to successful operations like the Termoli landing, and by the end of the month the US Fifth and BR Eighth armies had established a continuous front north of Naples and north of Foggia. It was at this point that Hitler made his mind up, and ordered his units to defend for as long as possible. The decision, suggested by Generalfeldmarschall Albert Kesselring, offered many advantages, such as the possibility of defending the narrowest part of Italy – the Gaeta–Ortona line – with just a dozen divisions. In order to accomplish this aim, the Bernhardt Line was built, followed by a second defensive line centred around the town of Cassino, which was named Gustav.

In November 1943, the Allied armies had not yet attempted to overcome any of the German defensive lines. US Fifth Army halted at the Mignano Gap, across which ran Highway 6 to Rome, while BR Eighth Army was preparing to cross the Sangro River. The plan was for the latter to advance

Soldiers of the 36th 'Texas' Division amongst the ruins of San Pietro. This kind of scene would soon become typical of the Italian campaign. (Keystone/Hulton Archive/ Getty Images)

along the Adriatic coast and then turn west, attacking the German positions from the rear, while the former advanced towards Rome. The 'Winter Line' – the name given by the Allies to the Bernhardt Line – was not considered insurmountable, and the hope was that Rome could be seized before Christmas 1943.

As Generalfeldmarschall Kesselring took command in Italy, determined to hold ground at all costs, the Germans were now set for a stubborn defence of the Bernhardt Line, with the aim of halting the Allied advance and completing the Gustav Line. The battles fought in December 1943 would be decisive for the future of the Italian campaign.

In December 1943, the Allied arms unleashed their attacks, which resulted in hard, prolonged and costly battles never seen before. In the US Fifth Army area the Americans fought hard at San Pietro, while in the BR Eighth Army sector the New Zealanders struggled to seize the key town of Orsogna. Eventually, as the Canadians fought a house-by-house struggle at Ortona, the outcome of the Winter Line campaign had become clear. By the end of 1943, the Allied two-pronged attack on Rome had failed, leaving US Fifth Army to advance towards Rome and fight at Cassino and Anzio. Rome would be seized before Christmas – but not until 1944.

CHRONOLOGY

1943

3 September	BR Eighth Army lands in Calabria.
8–9 September	Allied landing at Salerno, surrender of Italy. BR V Corps landing at Taranto.
17 September	German withdrawal to the Volturno Line.
1 October	US Fifth Army enters Naples.
3 October	Commandos and BR 78th Infantry Division land at Termoli, and face German counter-attacks.
12 October	US Fifth Army starts its offensive on the Volturno River.
13 October	The Kingdom of Italy declares war on Nazi Germany. German forces start their withdrawal to the Barbara Line.
26 October	US Fifth Army attacks the Barbara Line, which the Germans have abandoned.
31 October	US 3rd Division advances to the Mignano Gap.
1 November	Generalfeldmarschall Kesselring orders his forces to hold the Bernhardt (Winter) Line until the Gustav Line is complete.
4 November	US 504th Parachute Infantry Regiment (PIR) seizes Isernia, linking the US 5th and BR Eighth armies.
5 November	BR X Corps reaches the Garigliano River, US VI Corps reaches the Sangro River and the Winter Line, halting to rest ten days later.
20 November	BR V Corps crosses the Sangro River, starting BR Eighth Army's offensive.
2–3 December	NZ 2nd Division attacks Orsogna, heavily defended by the Germans. US 1st Special Service Force (SSF) and US 36th Division attack Mount Camino.
5 December	CDN 1st Infantry Division crosses the Moro River and begins its advance, along with IND 8th Division, towards Ortona.
7–8 December	Canadian attack towards Ortona, and New Zealander second attack against Orsogna.
8 December	US 36th Division attacks San Pietro.
14 December	The bulk of German 1.Fallschirmjäger-Division is redeployed in the Ortona area.
15 December	Second American attack against San Pietro, third New Zealander attack against Orsogna.
17 December	Following the German withdrawal, US 36th Division seizes San Pietro.
20–21 December	CDN 1st Infantry Division commences its attack against Ortona.
21 December	US Fifth Army approaches the German defensive line west of San Pietro and starts its offensive towards the Gustav Line.
24 December	Last New Zealander attack against Orsogna.
28 December	German troops withdraw from Ortona, which is in Canadian control.
30 December	General Bernard Montgomery relinquishes command of BR Eighth Army to General Oliver Leese; the British advance comes to a halt.

1944

1 January	US Fifth Army attacks to approach the Liri River valley.
12 January	French Expeditionary Corps starts its offensive north of Cassino.
17 January	BR X Corps crosses the Garigliano River.
20–21 January	US 36th Division crosses the Rapido River. Start of the battle for Cassino.

OPPOSING COMMANDERS

ALLIED

The Winter Line campaign comprised a series of small-unit engagements, with field commanders at the forefront of the battles. **Major-General Geoffrey T. Keyes,** the experienced commander of US II Corps, from 18 November 1943 controlled both the US 3rd and the 36th divisions. Keyes graduated at West Point in 1913, and three years later took part in the Punitive Expedition to Mexico. In 1941, after serving as Chief of Staff to the 2nd Armored Division under General George S. Patton, he led a Combat Command of US 3rd Armored Division. In 1942, Keyes formed and headed the US 9th Armored Division, before becoming deputy commander of the US Seventh Army. Again under Patton, during the invasion of Sicily he was given command of a provisional army corps that swept the eastern part of the island. He led the US II Corps from September 1943 to the end of the Italian campaign, in which his name became closely associated with the infamous Rapido River crossing. He retired in 1954, and died in 1967 aged 79.

    Major-General Fred L. Walker led the US 36th Division commander, and his name also became associated with the Rapido River crossing. Walker

Major-General Geoffrey T. Keyes (right), portrayed here along with US Seventh Army's commander Lieutenant-General George S. Patton (left), at Presenzano, Italy, January 1944. (NARA via Digital History Archive)

had his first experience of the Italian campaign during the Salerno landings, which enabled him to familiarize himself with the environment. Commissioned in 1911, he had also taken part in the expedition to Mexico, before serving on the Western Front in World War I. Wounded and decorated with the DSO, in September 1941 Walker took command of the all-Texas US 36th Infantry Division, a position he held until July 1944, in spite of him being the oldest divisional commander in the US Army. Having returned stateside, he was given command of the Infantry School at Fort Benning before becoming Director of Military Training with the Army Service Forces. Following his retirement in 1946, Walker was instrumental in beginning the congressional investigation into the Rapido River crossing. He led the Texas National Guard until 1948, and died in 1969 aged 82.

Lieutenant-General Charles W. Allfrey, the commander of BR V Corps, co-led the NZ 2nd Division during the Battle of Orsogna alongside the BR XIII Corps commander Lieutenant-General Miles C. Dempsey. Although educated at the Royal Naval College, in 1914 Allfrey was commissioned in the Royal Artillery and earned a Military Cross

Major-General Fred L. Walker, the renowned US 36th Infantry Division commander, awards the Silver Star to Staff-Sergeant Howard Graham, of Salem, Virginia. (NARA via Digital History Archive)

fighting in World War I. After various appointments, Allfrey attended the Staff College and was promoted colonel before joining the staff of BR 2nd Division. He witnessed combat in 1940, and commanded a brigade and a division until promoted to acting lieutenant-general in May 1942. Placed in command of BR V Corps, Allfrey fought in the Tunisian and the Italian campaigns until March 1944. He was then sent to Egypt, where he remained until his retirement in 1948. He died in 1964 aged 69.

Dempsey's career was more conventional. Commissioned in 1915, he, too, served in France, where he was wounded and was awarded the Military Cross. After attending the War College, he served with the War Office, with the BR 6th Division in Palestine, and as a brigade commander in France in 1940. Promoted major-general in 1941, he was given command of BR XIII Corps in November 1942 at Montgomery's request. After the Tunisian and Italian campaigns, in December 1943 Dempsey followed Montgomery to Britain where he took command of BR Second Army, which he led until May 1945 before transferring to head the BR Fourteenth Army in South-East Asia. In 1946, Dempsey was made Commander-in-Chief Middle East, retiring that same year. He died in 1969 aged 73.

Lieutenant-General Sir Bernard Freyberg epitomizes New Zealand's participation in the war against the Axis. Born in Britain and having emigrated to New Zealand as a child, he fought in World War I (most notably at Gallipoli), earning a DSO and the Victoria Cross. Compelled to retire on medical grounds in 1937, shortly after his promotion to major-general, in 1939 he succeeded in returning to duty and joined the New Zealand Army, being given command of the NZ 2nd Division. His division fought in 1941 in Greece and Crete, between 1941 and 1943 in North Africa, and between 1943 and 1945 in Italy. Appointed Governor General of New Zealand in 1946, he returned to Britain in 1952, and died in 1963 aged 74.

A prominent figure in Canadian military history, the Irish-born **Major-General Christopher Vokes** was commissioned in 1925, joining the Royal Canadian Engineers in the relatively small permanent force. Vokes's military career took off in 1939, with the army's expansion following the outbreak of war. First a staff officer with the CDN 1st Infantry Division, he commanded the Princess Patricia's Canadian Light Infantry (PPCLI) regiment. Promoted brigadier in June 1942, he was given command of CDN 2nd Infantry Brigade; after the campaign in Sicily and southern Italy, on 1 November 1943 Vokes was promoted major-general and given command of CDN 1st Infantry Division, which he led until the end of November 1944. After commanding the CDN 4th Armoured Division in North-West Europe, Vokes headed the short-lived Canadian Army Occupation Force until 1946. He retired in 1959, and died in 1985 aged 81.

AXIS

A classic portrait of Generalleutnant Frido von Senger und Etterlin who, as commander of XIV.Panzer-Korps, would acquire fame soon after the Winter Line battles as the defender of Monte Cassino. (Public domain)

Generalleutnant Frido (Fridolin) von Senger und Etterlin, commander of XIV. Panzer-Korps, studied at St John's College in Oxford before beginning his military career. After serving on the Western Front and fighting in the post-war volunteer corps, in 1920 von Senger joined the Reichswehr, switching from artillery to cavalry. In 1940, he took part in the invasion of the Netherlands, then served in the staff of the armistice commission with France until given command of 17.Panzer-Division in October 1942. He was a liaison officer with the Italian Sixth Army in Sicily from June 1943, and headed the German units on the island until appointed commander of Corsica. Following the successful withdrawal to mainland Italy, in October he replaced General von Hube as commander of XIV.Panzer-Korps, which he led until the end of the war. Instrumental in the creation of the post-war Bundeswehr, he had a prominent role in the Federal Republic of Germany until his death in 1963, aged 72.

General der Panzertruppe Traugott Herr, commander of LXXVI.Panzer-Korps, was commissioned in 1911. After fighting in World War I, he joined the Reichswehr in 1919. Involved in the motorization of the army from 1925, Herr was a regiment and brigade commander with 13.Infanterie- (then Panzer-) Division until given provisional command of the unit in December 1941. After distinguishing himself on the Eastern Front, in April 1942 Herr was promoted Generalmajor and given command of 13.Panzer-Division, which he held until severely wounded on 31 October 1942. After his recovery, in June 1943 he was given command of the newly formed LXXVI.Panzer-Korps, which he held (apart from between March and April 1944, when replaced by General von Choltitz) until December 1944. After a brief period in command of AOK 14, Herr was hospitalized until February 1945 and then given command of Armee Oberkommando (AOK) 10. Released in 1948, he died in 1976 aged 85.

Units from several other divisions faced the Allied attacks dealt with in this work. At San Pietro Infine, both the 15. and 29.Panzergrenadier-Division were involved. The former was commanded by **Generalleutnant Eberhard Rodt.** He was born in 1895 and volunteered for service in World War I. After fighting in the Freikorps, in 1920 he joined the Reichswehr, commanding cavalry units once more. In 1939, he commanded the Aufklärungs-Abteilung of 25.Infanterie-Division and fought in the West, earning the Ritterkreuz (Knight's Cross). Attached to 2.Panzer-Division the following autumn, he led its infantry on the Eastern Front until joining the reserve in October 1942. Given command of 22.Panzer-Division that November, he was promoted Generalmajor in March 1943. In May, he was given command of Division-Sizilien (then 15.Panzergrenadier-Division), which he led in Italy and on the Western Front until the end of the war (apart from between October and November 1944, when he suffered a car accident). Released in 1946, he died in 1979 aged 84.

General der Panzertruppe Traugott Herr, LXXVI.Panzer-Korps' commander from June 1943 to December 1944. Shortly after the end of Eighth Army's offensive on the Adriatic front, Herr led the German counter-offensive at Anzio. (Photo by Heinrich Hoffmann/ ullstein bild via Getty Images)

Generalleutnant Walter Fries, commander of 29.Panzergrenadier-Division, was born in 1894. An army volunteer from 1912, he was commissioned three years later and, after World War I, joined the police until 1936, when he returned to army service. After fighting in Poland and the West as a battalion commander, in November 1940 he was given command of Infanterie-Regiment (mot.) 87, fighting on the Eastern Front. In March 1943, he was appointed to command the rebuilt 29.Panzergrenadier-Division which he led in Italy, earning promotion to Generalleutnant, as well as the Eichenlaub (Oak Leaves) to the Ritterkreuz. From September 1944, he led XXXXVI. Panzer-Korps. Promoted General der Panzertruppe in December, in March 1945, after the fall of 'Fortress Warsaw', Fries was relieved of command and put under trial, eventually escaping the death penalty. Released in 1947, he died in 1982 aged 86.

Generalleutnant Richard 'Arno' Heidrich, born in 1896, volunteered for the army in 1914 and was commissioned in 1915. In spite of his bravery and injury, Heidrich was not promoted, but managed to join the Reichswehr in 1920. Shortly after his promotion to Major in 1936, he joined the Fallschirm-Infanterie-Kompanie, and three years later took command of the Fallschirm-Infanterie-Bataillon. Transferred to the Luftwaffe in 1939, he commanded II./Fallschirmjäger-Regiment 1 before joining the staff of 7.Flieger-Division. Given command of Fallschirmjäger-Regiment 3 in May 1940, he fought in the Netherlands and on Crete, and later on the Eastern Front. Promoted Generalmajor and given command of 7.Flieger- (from June 1943, 1.Fallschirmjäger-) Division in August 1942, he led it on Sicily and the Italian mainland until June 1944, when he took command of I.Fallschirm-

One of the most distinguished veterans of the German Fallschirmjäger, Generalleutnant Richard Heidrich (right) fought with 7.Flieger-Division (later 1.Fallschirjäger-Division) in the Netherlands, on Crete, on the Eastern Front and in Italy. (Wikimedia)

Korps. Promoted General der Fallschirmtruppe in October, in January 1945 he relinquished command after being severely wounded. He died in hospital in 1947, aged 51.

Generalleutnant Smilo Freiherr von Lüttwitz, born in 1895, was commissioned in 1914. His career in the post-war Reichswehr showed relatively rapid progress, taking command of Aufklärungs-Abteilung (mot.) 5 in October 1936. A staff officer in 1939, in May 1940 he was given command of Schützen-Regiment 12, fighting on the Western and Eastern fronts. Given command of 23.Infanterie-Division in July 1942, in September he was promoted Generalmajor and given command of 26.Panzer-Division. From July 1944 he headed XXXXVI.Panzer-Korps, before being replaced at the end of August by Walter Fries. He was promoted General der Panzertruppe in September and given command of AOK 9. Relieved from command by Generalfeldmarschall Schörner, he was put on trial but was acquitted of all charges. He then led LXXXV.Armee-Korps between April and May 1945, and after his release from Allied captivity he joined the Bundeswehr commanding its III.Korps until retirement in 1960. He died in 1975, aged 80.

Generalmajor Hellmuth Pfeifer, born in 1894, was commissioned in 1913 and fought in World War I as an infantry officer before joining the Reichswehr. After several stints as a company commander, in 1937 he joined the Oberkommando der Wehrmacht as a staff officer until given command of an infantry battalion in 1939. A regimental commander after the campaign in the West, he fought on the Eastern Front, being promoted Generalmajor in September 1943. He led 65.Infanterie-Division from December that year, and distinguished himself during the June 1944 withdrawal, being awarded the Eichenlaub to the Ritterkreuz. Whilst still in command of the division, Hellmuth Pfeifer was killed on 22 April 1945 north of Bologna.

OPPOSING FORCES

ALLIED

The strategic uncertainty about the campaign in Italy and the predominance of Operation *Overlord* greatly influenced the composition of the Allied armies present on the peninsula, up to the battles for the Winter Line. Following the end of the Sicilian campaign, a grand total of six divisions were sent to Britain. This left (from September 1943) the US Fifth Army with one US corps (II, committed from 18 November) and one British corps, and a total of four American and two British infantry divisions. The only armoured unit, BR 7th Division, was withdrawn from the front in November and sent back to Britain, being replaced with the US 1st Armored Division. The US Fifth Army would only be reinforced until January 1944 by a Free French unit, the 2nd Moroccan Division, which arrived at the front in mid-December 1943 at the head of the French Expeditionary Corps.

BR Eighth Army would provide most of the units deployed in the US Fifth Army area, itself receiving no reinforcements. In September 1943, the BR XIII Corps was advancing from Messina on Italy's toe, with the BR 5th and CDN 1st Infantry divisions. The BR 1st Airborne Division, spearheading the BR V Corps, after landing at Taranto and seizing Foggia was followed by the 78th British and 8th Indian divisions at the end of September. Early in October, BR 1st Airborne Division was withdrawn from the front and sent back to Britain, following the arrival in Italy of NZ 2nd Division. Excluding the BR 1st Infantry Division, which landed at Anzio, by January 1944 British army strength in Italy had been increased only thanks to non-British units. By then, one Canadian armoured division (and the Canadian corps staff), one Indian and two Polish divisions with the Polish Corps had joined BR Eighth Army.

US infantry load a pack mule with .30-cal. light machine guns. This kind of transportation, extremely useful in Italy, came into its own in the winter of 1943. (NARA via Digital History Archive)

Infantry from the US 3rd Infantry Division in the ruins of Mignano, after its seizure. This was the kind of terrain infantrymen had to fight for, all too often in challenging weather conditions. (NARA via Digital History Archive)

The most obvious consequence on the Winter Line campaign was the near impossibility of rotating units, and both the US 5th and the BR Eighth armies only had one division in reserve throughout December 1943. This situation limited the Allied offensive capabilities since, as a general rule, each division only engaged two of its three infantry regiments (or the British equivalent brigades) at a time, in order to rotate them. This only partly explains why Allied units, which were stronger on paper than their German counterparts, faced so many difficulties against an all too often inferior enemy. Moreover, Allied units suffered from an unfavourable 'tooth-to-tail' ratio.

The 1942 American 'triangular' (i.e. with three infantry regiments) division had an overall strength of about 15,370 men. Its armaments included 12 155mm and 36 105mm howitzers in three artillery battalions, the latter usually split amongst the infantry regiments forming Regimental Combat Teams (RCTs). The core of the RCT was the infantry regiment, about 3,470 strong, which was armed with 189 Browning Automatic Rifles, 18 light .30-cal. and 24 heavy .30-cal. machine guns (plus ten .50-cal. machine guns), 27 light 60mm and 18 heavy 81mm mortars, plus 24 37mm anti-tank guns. The problem was that the three infantry regiments could be supported by other divisional units (reconnaissance, engineers) only when suitable conditions permitted, and often they were the only units carrying out the assault.

Interestingly, such impressive US firepower was not matched by adequate infantry strength. Each of the three infantry battalions in the regiment was 912 strong, with each of its three rifle companies having 198 men, the heavy weapons company having 183. This meant that only 777 men (594 excluding the heavy weapons company) would actually be fighting in a single battalion, or 2,331 (1,782 riflemen) in each of the three regiments. It is worth noting that the sum of the infantry combat strength of the three regiments (6,993, or 5,346 riflemen) amounted to about 45 per cent of the total infantry strength. As a result, even limited losses – usually absorbed in their entirety by the rifle and, to an extent, the heavy weapons companies – could result in a severe reduction of the actual fighting strength of a single US division.

Unsurprisingly, firepower (usually increased by corps artillery and air force support) was considered essential in the attack, while only a limited number of infantry units would be deployed. The tactics were based on the 'two up, one back' principle, which saw two of the three rifle companies being used in the attack, and the third being held back. This led to avoiding (unless absolutely necessary) frontal attacks against enemy-held positions, favouring envelopment instead.

A Canadian crew firing a Mk II 3in. (81.2mm) mortar. Heavy infantry weapons, mortars in particular, provided essential support to the riflemen during the attack. (NARA via Digital History Archive)

Both the Canadian and the New Zealand divisions were structured like the British infantry divisions, both countries being part of the Commonwealth and adhering to the same organization. Despite being more centralized and stronger in terms of manpower (with an overall strength of about 18,300), the Canadian division shared the same issues as its American counterpart. A 1943 Canadian infantry division had three rifle brigades, each with three rifle battalions plus a machine-gun battalion in support.[1] Overall firepower saw a total of 72 25-pdr field guns, 16 anti-tank and 54 Bofors anti-aircraft guns in the divisional artillery units. On the other hand, with an overall strength of about 2,900 (fewer than the 2,500 for the New Zealand Division), the infantry brigade was considerably weaker than the US RCT. As a matter of fact, in British and Commonwealth units the focus was not on the brigade, which basically comprised a staff controlling the rifle battalions, but on the individual rifle battalions.

Reorganized in May 1944, a Canadian rifle battalion had an overall strength of 848; its New Zealand counterpart had just 776 men. Each battalion had a support company armed with heavy machine guns and mortars, plus four rifle companies. The Canadian ones were only 127 strong, but this still achieved a higher percentage of combat strength than its American counterpart (about 52 per cent of the entire divisional infantry), bearing in mind too that the rifle battalion possessed more firepower. This included 63 light machine guns, 23 Projector Infantry Anti-Tank (PIAT) anti-tank guns, 26 light and six heavy mortars, and six 6-pdr anti-tank guns (a US infantry battalion had 45 Browning Automatic Rifles, 12 light machine guns, nine light and six heavy mortars and four anti-tank guns).

The New Zealand division, suffering a greater manpower shortage than its Canadian and American counterparts, had inferior numbers. After the

1   The regiment was in fact an administrative entity, formed of one or more battalions which were grouped in brigades to avoid confusion. It is worth noting that the Canadians named their regiments in the same fashion as the British Army; the New Zealand Army numbered its regiments instead.

Bringing supplies to the front line was a problem in the early phase of the Italian campaign, fuel transportation in particular. (NARA via Digital History Archive)

A 20mm Flakvierling in position in Italy, December 1943. It is worth noting, as shown here, that in the winter of 1943/44 German soldiers were still wearing tropical uniforms. (Keystone-France/Gamma-Keystone via Getty Images)

heavy losses suffered at El Alamein, the NZ 4th Infantry Brigade was withdrawn and reorganized as an armoured brigade with three tank battalions and a motor battalion, which was 761 strong. The NZ 2nd Division was thus an infantry unit with a mixed organization, its overall strength totalling about 16,800. One of the consequences of the reduced strength was that each New Zealand battalion was just 776 strong (a brigade being 2,479 strong). Since the division only had six of them, the New Zealanders were more likely to suffer from attrition. Tank support was provided by both the American and Canadian divisions' attached units.

In spite of its inferior numbers, the NZ 2nd Division was the most experienced of the three taken into account here. Formed, like the CDN 1st Infantry Division, immediately following the outbreak of war in September 1939, the NZ 2nd Division was sent to Egypt in January 1940 and subsequently redeployed to Greece where, in April 1941, it had its baptism of fire. Following the withdrawal from Crete in May, the division was sent to North Africa, where it took part in the November 1941 Operation *Crusader* and, in 1942, the battles at Mersa Matruh and El Alamein. After fighting in Tunisia, with just two brigades, the division was reorganized and sent to Italy.

The CDN 1st Infantry Division was sent to the United Kingdom in December 1939, and, while some of its units were individually engaged (at Dieppe, for example), the division did not have its baptism of fire until the landing in Sicily in July 1943. At the end of the Sicilian campaign the division was reorganized, and sent to Italy. Formed in 1940 entirely in Texas at Camp Bowie from the National Guard, the US 36th Infantry Division was subsequently trained at Camp Blanding, Florida, and Camp Edwards, Massachusetts before taking part in the 1941 manoeuvres in Louisiana. Sent to North Africa in April 1943, the division first tasted combat during the Salerno landings in September (when overstrength in infantry); after rest and refit, it returned to the line by mid-November, now with about 75–80 per cent of its established strength.

AXIS

Until Generalfeldmarschall Kesselring took over in November 1943, German forces in Italy were split in two with General Rommel commanding Heeresgruppe (HGr) B in northern Italy, and Kesselring in command in the south. As a result, it was not until

December 1943 that units were redeployed from northern Italy, limiting the number of German divisions facing the Allied armies.

Most of the units under Kesselring's command were an odd mixture; some had been formed from the remnants of the Deutsches Afrika Korps, others were rebuilt after being destroyed at Stalingrad. Units intended for the 15.Panzer-Division, including Panzergrenadier-Regiment 129 (attached until the end of the year) were used to form Division Sizilien, renamed 15.Panzergrenadier-Division in July 1943. Likewise,

90.Panzergrenadier-Division was formed in September 1943 from the Kommando Sardinien, made up of remnants from 90.leichte-Afrika-Division. Partly destroyed in Tunisia, the Fallschirm-Panzer-Division 'Hermann Göring' was rebuilt in Sicily.

The 16.Panzer-Division, 3.Panzergrenadier-Division as well as the 29.Panzergrenadier-Division had been destroyed at Stalingrad in 1942–43 and rebuilt. A few units were newly formed, such as the 65.Infanterie- and 26.Panzer-Division, organized in France in July and September 1942 and sent to Italy in summer 1943. The 1.Fallschirmjäger-Division, the best and most experienced unit, was formed in May 1943 by re-designating 7.Flieger-Division, and was also employed in Sicily in July 1943.

As a result, most German units were not up to their established strength and their organization varied greatly. A 1943 *Panzergrenadier-Division* was to have a four-company *Panzer-Bataillon*, two *Panzergrenadier-Regimenter*, each one with three battalions, one *Artillerie-Regiment* with three battalions (one of which was self-propelled), plus Flak, Panzerjäger, Pionier and Aufklärungs battalions. Overall strength was about 13,900, which was seldom achieved. A *Panzer-Division* was intended to have a two-battalion *Panzer-Regiment* (one equipped with Panther, the other with Panzer IV tanks), two *Panzergrenadier-Regimenter*, each with two battalions, plus a three-battalion *Artillerie-Regiment*, along with Flak, Panzerjäger, Pionier and Aufklärungs battalions. Overall strength was to be 13,700. The two-regiment *Infanterie-Division* had three infantry battalions in each *Infanterie-Regiment*, and one *Artillerie-Regiment* with four battalions. The division also had a Panzerjäger and a Pionier battalion, plus a rifle (Füsilier) batallion acting as divisional reconnaissance unit. Overall strength was set at 12,350.

In October 1943, 15.Panzergrenadier-Division reported six *Panzergrenadier-Bataillone* with an actual strength of 27 per cent, and two others at 34 and 38 per cent. The divisional *Panzer-Abteilung* had 23 Panzer IV tanks and 21 Sturmgeschütz self-propelled guns. Early in November, 3.Panzergrenadier-Division was in similarly poor shape. One battalion had 8 per cent of its establishment, another 16 per cent, two

Riflemen of the Canadian Queen's Royal Regiment dug in at Mount Camino in December 1943. The photo is revealing of the challenging conditions these soldiers had to endure during the Winter Line campaign. (NARA via Digital History Archive)

36–37 per cent and only one close to 50 per cent of the establishment. On 10 November, 26.Panzer-Division reported its four *Panzergrenadier-Bataillone* as having a total combat strength of 1,336 all ranks. The 15.Panzergrenadier-Division's combat strength, including its three regiments, was 3,663 all ranks, the *Panzergrenadier-Regimenter* having now on average 70 per cent of their established strength.

The 1.Fallschirmjäger-Division – which included three *Fallschirmjäger-Regimenter*, each with three battalions; one three-battalion *Fallschirm-Artillerie-Regiment* (equipped with light guns); plus Fallschirm-Maschinengehwer (machine-gun), Panzerjäger and Pionier battalions – recovered its strength quickly. Early in October, it reported a total combat strength of 1,300 all ranks, but in December, when the total combat strength of Fallschirmjäger-Regiment 3 and Fallschirmjäger-Regiment 4 in the Ortona area was about 1,200 all ranks, the division reported a total strength of 11,864 all ranks – close to full strength.

At the tactical level, German units were stronger than their American counterparts and roughly equivalent to the Canadian and New Zealand ones. A *Panzergrenadier-Division* regiment, like the *Panzer-Division* one, featured support companies: Infanterie-Geschütz (infantry gun), Panzerjäger and Flak. However, a *Panzergrenadier-Division* and a *Panzer-Division Panzergrenadier-Bataillon* were different, since the former had four infantry companies plus support, while the latter had three infantry and one heavy weapon companies, plus support. Therefore, a three-battalion *Panzergrenadier-Regiment* was 3,043 strong and had six anti-tank, 12 infantry and eight anti-aircraft guns in the support companies. Each of its battalions (868 strong) had 72 light and 12 heavy machine guns, eight medium mortars and 12 anti-tank guns.

A two-battalion *Panzergrenadier-Regiment* would be weaker numerically (2,294 all ranks), but its battalions could be compared to those in the *Panzergrenadier-Division* being 867 strong, and having 60 light and 12 heavy machine guns, six medium and four heavy mortars and nine light

and three heavy anti-tank guns. A single company, 183 strong, would have 18 light and four heavy machine guns, two medium mortars and three anti-tank weapons (at the time the old anti-tank rifles were being replaced by rocket launchers). The heavy weapons company had six light machine guns, six flame-throwers, four heavy mortars and three anti-tank guns.

The German infantry units were weaker, with a 2,008-strong, three-battalion *Infanterie-Regiment*, armed with 107 light and 24 heavy machine guns, 12 medium and eight heavy mortars and eight infantry and three anti-tank guns. A standard *Infanterie-Kompanie* was armed with 12 light machine guns and two medium mortars, the heavy weapons company

having 12 heavy machine guns and three heavy mortars. Considering a total of 36 light and 12 heavy machine guns, six medium and three heavy mortars the *Infanterie-Bataillon* was a rather weak unit.

Albeit relatively, the *Fallschirmäger-Regiment*, with 3,200 men, was the strongest and best-armed unit as it had 224 light and 24 heavy machine guns, 39 light and 12 medium mortars and three anti-tank guns. The same applied to the *Fallschirmjäger-Bataillon*, whose three basic companies were each armed with 20 light machine guns, three anti-tank guns and three light mortars. The machine-gun company had eight heavy machine guns, four medium mortars and two 75mm infantry guns. The total for each *Fallschirmjäger-Bataillon* was impressive: 60 light and eight heavy machine guns, nine light and four medium mortars and nine anti-tank and two infantry guns.

On 1 October 1943, the total strength of AOK 10 was about 60,440 all ranks, XIV.Panzer-Korps standing at some 33,780 and LXXVI.Panzer-Korps 24,780 men. Replacements, and reinforcements from northern Italy (94., 44. and 305.Infanterie-Division, and 29.Panzergrenadier-Division) saw AOK 10's strength rise to 141,634 all ranks on 9 December. Even though part of this force was deployed behind the front (such as the 26,800 Luftwaffe combat personnel, mostly in Flak units), it is clear how by the end of 1943 the Germans had managed to rebalance their strength compared with the Allied armies. This enabled them to fully exploit the advantage they held of defending on favourable terrain.

Private Morris Schimmel, from Clayton, Missouri, inspects the wreck of a Sturmgeschütz III. The battles of San Pietro, Orsogna and Ortona demonstrated how an Allied superiority in armour did not suffice to overcome the German defences. (NARA via Digital History Archive)

ORDERS OF BATTLE

ALLIED, DECEMBER 1943

Commander in Chief, Allied Forces Headquarters: General Dwight D. Eisenhower (from 27 December, effective 14 January 1944, General Sir Henry Maitland Wilson)

15TH ARMY GROUP (GENERAL SIR HAROLD ALEXANDER)

US Fifth Army (Lieutenant-General Mark W. Clark)
BR 7th Armoured Division (to Britain, replaced on 15 November by:)
US 1st Armored Division (Major-General Ernest N. Harmon) (on 27 December, 6th Armored Infantry Regiment in line with 3rd Division)
BR X Corps (Lieutenant-General Richard L. McCreery)
    BR 46th Infantry Division (Major-General John L. I. Hawkesworth)
        BR 128th Infantry Brigade
        BR 138th Infantry Brigade
        BR 139th Infantry Brigade
    BR 56th Infantry Division (Major-General Gerald W.R. Templer)
        BR 167th Infantry Brigade
        BR 169th Infantry Brigade
        BR 201st Guards Infantry Brigade
US II Corps (Major-General Geoffrey T. Keyes)
    US 36th Infantry Division (Major-General Fred L. Walker) – see separate 'San Pietro' order of battle
    US 3rd Infantry Division (Major-General Lucian K. Truscott, Jr.)
        US 7th Regimental Combat Team
        US 15th Regimental Combat Team
        US 30th Regimental Combat Team
US VI Corps (Major-General John P. Lucas)
    US 45th Infantry Division (Major-General Troy H. Middleton)
        US 157th Regimental Combat Team
        US 179th Regimental Combat Team
        US 180th Regimental Combat Team
    US 34th Infantry Division (Major-General Charles W. Ryder)
        US 133rd Regimental Combat Team
        US 135th Regimental Combat Team
        US 168th Regimental Combat Team
    FR 2nd Moroccan Infantry Division (Général de Division André Dody) (replaced US 34th Division on 9–13 December)
        FR 4th Moroccan Infantry Regiment
        FR 5th Moroccan Infantry Regiment
        FR 8th Moroccan Infantry Regiment

BR Eighth Army (General Sir Bernard L. Montgomery)
Arriving in December:
    CDN 5th Armoured Division
    IND 4th Infantry Division
    BR 1st Infantry Division
BR XIII Corps (Lieutenant-General Miles C. Dempsey)
    CDN 1st Infantry Division (Major-General Christopher Vokes) (11 December to BR V Corps) – see separate 'Ortona' order of battle
    BR 5th Infantry Division (Major-General Gerard C. Bucknall)
        BR 13th Infantry Brigade
        BR 15th Infantry Brigade
        BR 17th Infantry Brigade
BR V Corps (Lieutenant-General Charles W. Allfrey)
    NZ 2nd Division (Lieutenant-General Sir Bernard Freyberg) (16 December to BRXIII Corps) – see separate 'Orsogna' order of battle
    IND 8th Division (Major-General Dudley Russell)
        IND 17th Indian Infantry Brigade
        IND 19th Indian Infantry Brigade
        IND 21st Indian Infantry Brigade
    BR 78th British Infantry Division (Major-General Vyvyan Evelegh) (to reserve from 11 December, then to BR XIII Corps)
        BR 11th Infantry Brigade
        BR 36th Infantry Brigade
        BR 38th Infantry Brigade
BR 4th Armoured Brigade

AXIS, DECEMBER 1943

HEERESGRUPPE C/OBERBEFEHLSHABER SÜDWEST (GENERALFELDMARSCHALL ALBERT KESSELRING)

AOK 10 (General der Panzertruppe Heinrich von Vietinghoff to 24 October; from 1 November temporarily General der Panzertruppe Joachim Lemelsen)
5.Gebirgs-Division (Generalleutnant Julius Ringel)
    Gebirgsjäger-Regiment 85
    Gebirgsjäger-Regiment 100
Fallschirm-Panzer-Division 'Hermann Göring' (Generalleutnant Paul Conrath)
    Panzergrenadier-Regiment 1 'Hermann Göring'
    Panzergrenadier-Regiment 2 'Hermann Göring'
    Panzer-Regiment 1 'Hermann Göring'
XIV.Panzer-Korps (General der Panzertruppe Hans-Valentin Hube to 24 October, from 28 October Generalleutnant Fridolin von Senger und Etterlin)
    94.Infanterie-Division (Generalleutnant Georg Pfeiffer)
        Grenadier-Regiment 267
        Grenadier-Regiment 274
        Grenadier-Regiment 276
    15.Panzergrenadier-Division (Generalleutnant Eberhard Rodt) – see separate 'San Pietro' order of battle
    29.Panzergrenadier-Division (Generalleutnant Walter Fries) – see separate 'San Pietro' order of battle
    44.Infanterie-Division (Generalleutnant Dr Franz Beyer)
        Grenadier-Regiment 131
        Grenadier-Regiment 132
        Grenadier-Regiment 134
    305.Infanterie-Division (Generalleutnant Friedrich-Wilhelm Hauck)
        Grenadier-Regiment 576
        Grenadier-Regiment 577
        Grenadier-Regiment 578
LXXVI.Panzer-Korps (General der Panzertruppe Traugott Herr)
    1.Fallschirmjäger-Division (Generalleutnant Richard Heidrich) – see separate 'Orsogna/Ortona' order of battle
    26.Panzer-Division (Generalleutnant Smilo von Lüttwitz) – see separate 'Orsogna/Ortona' order of battle
    65.Infanterie-Division (Generalmajor Gustav Heistermann von Ziehlberg, from 1 December Generalmajor Hellmuth Pfeifer) – see separate 'Orsogna/Ortona' order of battle
    90.Panzergrenadier-Division (Generalleutnant Carl Hans Lungershausen, from 20 December Generalmajor Ernst-Günther Baade)
        Panzergrenadier-Regiment 155
        Panzergrenadier-Regiment 200
        Panzergrenadier-Regiment 361
    334.Infanterie-Division (Generalleutnant Walter Scheller from late December)
        Grenadier-Regiment 754
        Grenadier-Regiment 755
        Grenadier-Regiment 756

Note: further, more specific orders of battle are provided later in this work in the relevant battle narratives.

OPPOSING PLANS

ALLIED

The Allied strategy in the Mediterranean and in Italy was more the result of coincidence than intent. During the First Quebec Conference, codenamed 'Quadrant', which began on 12 August 1943 in Quebec, British plans for the development of a Mediterranean strategy were accepted, albeit to a limited extent, by the Americans, although maintaining Operation *Overlord* was prioritized. Faced with the collapse of Axis forces in Sicily, and Italy's request for an armistice, the planners considered an advance up the Italian boot to seize Naples and Rome, along with the capture of Sardinia and Corsica. For the first time, Allied strategy considered aims beyond the defeat of Italy.

Corporal Joseph P. Bisenius of the US 135th Infantry Regiment inspects the remains of a German vehicle near San Vittore. The reason for his wearing a bowler hat remains a mystery. (NARA via Digital History Archive)

Thanks to the seizure of strategic locations, such as the harbours at Naples and Taranto and the airports in the Foggia area, further operations in Italy would be aimed mostly at tying down German forces and preventing their deployment to North-West Europe. Territorial aims were limited, and, as the US Army Chief of Staff General George Marshall stated in August 1943 to General Dwight Eisenhower (commander of Allied Forces Headquarters), Allied strategy in Italy was aimed at seizing a line north of Rome. This, along with Sardinia and Corsica, would make an Allied landing in southern France possible.

For this purpose, Eisenhower was informed that 24 US, British (including Commonwealth and Imperial) and French divisions would be made available. Rome, with all its political and propaganda value, was the only real strategic goal to be accomplished in Italy, a point of view shared by Churchill. However, Eisenhower did not agree. In his view, restricting the Allied advance to an area just to the north of Rome would be impractical, and the Italian campaign could only end either with the Germans being driven out of the country, or the Allies forced to do the same. Most importantly, the actual divisional strengths put at disposal were not as important as the availability of personnel and materiel replacements, and of shipping and landing craft.

Most importantly, different assumptions lay behind these plans. The Combined Chiefs of Staff assumed that the Germans would defend Salerno and Taranto to the last man, in order to prevent any further Allied advances. As a result, when they withdrew from both as the Italians surrendered, many started to believe that the Germans would withdraw to northern Italy, up to the Alps. Amongst the latter were generals Eisenhower and Harold Alexander, the 15th Army Group commander, who planned the Italian campaign as a swift pursuit. Facing the seizure of Taranto and the German withdrawal from Salerno, it was believed that only a small force would be needed to seize Italy. While Marshall persisted with the plan to land in southern France, both American and British intelligence reckoned that the Germans would soon withdraw to central Italy (along a line running from Pisa to Rimini, running approximately along the 'Gothic Line' defences) leaving a covering force at Cassino. Therefore, a rapid advance seemed possible. The headquarters of Allied Armies in Italy (Alexander's command) prioritized the capture of strategic logistical and communication sites such as Naples and Foggia, reckoning that any further advance would be swift and easy.

By 17 September, Alexander was already convinced that the Germans would not hold southern Italy, and General Montgomery, BR Eighth Army's commander, was instructed to start preparations to advance to the Foggia–Termoli area by the end of September. The Combined Chiefs of Staff set no geographic objective in Italy, but on 21 September Alexander outlined a clear timetable for the Allied advance. By 7 October, Allied forces were to be in the Naples area, advancing by 7 November to Rome and by the end of the month to the line Lucca–Ravenna, which lay to the north of the Pisa–Rimini area. On 29 September, Alexander issued definitive plans; first, BR Eighth Army was to advance along the eastern, or Adriatic, coast reaching the area of Pescara with the aim of moving inland halfway towards Rome in the direction of Avezzano, beyond the central mountain range. The subsequent step would see US Fifth Army attack from the south, along the Route 6 highway from Cassino, aiming to break through the Liri Valley and advance to Frosinone, south-east of Rome. The pincer manoeuvre on the Eternal City would be completed by a amphibious landing to the south of Rome, which was to secure the Albano Hills just to the south.

At first sight the plan – clearly intended to break through the German defences, avoiding their concentration in a single area and an ensuing hard battle – was not without flaws. It clearly made Rome the objective of the Allied offensive, and at the same time failed to consider any other objective north of it. Still, the prevailing optimism clearly influenced planning. On 1 October, Eisenhower was still optimistic that his forces could be in Rome in six or eight weeks, and three days later he and Alexander agreed that this aim could

An M3 Stuart light tank moving along Route 6 in the Mount Lungo area. This road became the main aim of US Fifth Army, and eventually of the Allied forces in Italy, up to May 1944. (NARA via Digital History Archive)

be achieved within the month. One of the consequences of the prevailing optimism – soon to disappear when faced by the obvious German decision to hold their positions in southern Italy for as long as possible – was that Rome became the one and only goal of the Italian campaign. Both politicians and generals aimed at its seizure, without realizing that in the long run the Italian capital was of little value.

Most importantly, what was missing was a clear view of the situation, and of the German intentions and capabilities to withstand the Allied offensive. Alexander's 2 October directive to General Clark was to advance to the Sessa Aurunca–Isernia–Venafro line, with the clear aim of creating the basis for a subsequent advance into the Liri River valley. Clark, who along with his commanders was aware that the drive on Rome would not be a cake walk, realized at once what the problem would be: Cassino.

US Fifth Army's operational orders issued on 19 and 22 September called for a broad-front attack involving BR X Corps, which was given the main objective of seizing Naples, while the US VI Corps moved inland to the Volturno River. On 2 October, having been informed by Alexander of his optimistic plan to seize central Italy in a matter of months, Clark issued new orders shifting the main weight of US Fifth Army's attack to the US VI Corps sector, aiming to advance along the Volturno River valley. The BR X Corps would be confined to a stretch of land close to the Tyrrhenian coast, west of the Capua–Teano line. An amphibious landing in the Gulf of Gaeta, in the style of the Termoli landing, was also taken into account, but not planned for, because of the unsuitable beaches and of US VI Corps' advance.

In October, the Allied commanders eventually realized that the Germans would not be withdrawing to northern Italy, or the Alps. Nevertheless, the relatively easy advance of both the US 5th and BR Eighth armies suggested that a breakthrough was possible. On 8 November, Alexander's headquarters issued new directives which matched the timetable plan developed at the end of September. The first phase of the Allied offensive was to have the BR Eighth Army advance in the Pescara area and, if possible, to swing westwards towards Rome, threatening the German lines of communications. Ideally, such a threat would be enough to compel a German withdrawal to

A Sturmgeschütz III being towed away from the battle area at Mount Lungo, January 1944. The terrain was a predominant factor in the Italian campaign, and it prevented the Allies from exploiting their superiority in armour and materiel. (NARA via Digital History Archive)

the north of the Italian capital. The US Fifth Army would, in the second phase, advance to the Liri River valley towards Frosinone and, along with the third phase (an amphibious landing in the Rome area), complete the pincer movement on the Eternal City. Phase one, starting on 20 November, was intended to give the US Fifth Army time to regroup and prepare.

Realizing that only the seizure of the entrance to the Liri Valley – the 'gateway to Rome' – would permit the final aim of the plan to be achieved, Clark focused on the enemy positions directly in front of US Fifth Army. His 24 November orders required a triple-phase attack, starting with the seizure of the mountains at the bottom of the Liri Valley (Mount Camino, Mount La Difensa and Mount Maggiore), to be carried out by US II Corps in co-operation with BR X Corps. The latter would take over the positions seized after a feint to distract the enemy. The former was given the task, in phase two, of shifting north and seizing Mount Sammucro (north of San Pietro Infine), while the US VI Corps attacked to the north, along the mountains with the aim of reaching the heights to the north and the north-west of Cassino.

Once both shoulders of the Mignano Gap had been secured, phase three would commence with US VI Corps continuing its advance to the north and the north-west of Cassino. The US II Corps was to attack along Route 6, creating an armoured breakthrough, and BR X Corps was to advance along the coast. Ideally, US Fifth Army was to reach the line Fondi–Arce–Alvito just south of Frosinone, in the central area of the Liri Valley.

Logistical issues and the need to regroup his forces compelled Montgomery not to consider any advance towards Foggia before 1 October. Once preparations were complete, he intended to use the BR XIII Corps to seize Foggia while gathering forces in the Potenza area. Once the regrouping of BR V Corps was complete, it was to advance inland and protect BR XIII Corps' flank. The unexpected German withdrawal enabled Montgomery to seize Foggia on 27 September, but this did not make him change his plans. Once again, logistical and administrative issues delayed the advance, which Montgomery estimated could not be resumed until 21 October in spite of the successful landing at Termoli. On 9 November, as BR Eighth Army approached the Sangro River, Montgomery began planning his next move.

Mountainous terrain, the lack of good roads, the approaching winter and the fact that only one division could be used in the area led Montgomery to exclude an attack inland from Castel di Sangro. The same situation applied to the Atessa–Guardiagrele area, which Montgomery intended to use in order to support the main attack, which was to take place along the coastal road to Fossacesia and Ortona. Thus, the BR V Corps was to attack towards Pescara along the coastal road, while the NZ 2nd Division (directly under army command) was to attack towards Guardiagrele. The aim was to exert pressure on the town of Chieti while, inland, the BR XIII Corps was to carry out a diversionary attack along the line Alfedena–Castel di Sangro. The plan was outlined during a meeting on 8 November, which resulted in having BR Eighth Army deliver the main thrust while US Fifth Army was to keep the enemy forces engaged and seize key terrain.

On 25 October, Eisenhower informed the British Prime Minister Winston Churchill that in order to prevent the withdrawal of German units from Italy, the Allied armies were to maintain the initiative. In reply to his question as to whether Rome could be seized before January or February 1944, Churchill was told by the chiefs of staff that the capital could be seized before Christmas without an amphibious operation. He was also told that, should the latter prove necessary, no such operation could take place before January 1944.

AXIS

The key to the future German strategy and planning for the Italian campaign were the events of 8–9 September 1943. As the Italians surrendered, an Allied landing in the Rome area would have cut communications with AOK 10 in the south, making a withdrawal north of Rome necessary. Unsurprisingly, Kesselring's staff welcomed the Allied landing at Salerno with a sigh of relief.

Nevertheless, Axis strategy was still uncertain. Following Mussolini's downfall on 25 July 1943, he had deployed HGr B under Rommel's command in northern Italy, leaving Oberbefehlshaber Süd in the south, under Kesselring with AOK 10 and two corps. Still, in September Hitler intended to hand Rommel overall command in Italy, with the task of evacuating Sardinia and Corsica and withdrawing to northern Italy.

Most likely, Kesselring's 5 August reassurances to Hitler about the Italian willingness to continue to fight undermined his position. Not only was Rommel preferred, but Kesselring was also denied reinforcements. On the 14th, Kesselring offered his resignation, which Hitler refused, giving him new directives instead. He was to prepare a withdrawal to central Italy, taking into account a possible Allied landing, while defending the areas of Naples and Salerno. Only mobile forces would face the BR Eighth Army in Calabria. Rome was to be held until all the forces in southern Italy and Sardinia had been withdrawn.

On 3 September British forces landed in Calabria, followed six days later by the landings at Salerno and Taranto. The Italian surrender, announced on the evening of 8 September, led to a period of brief resistance (Rome capitulated two days later) and to the disarming of most of the Italian army. By 17 September, the Germans considered the situation secure with most of the mainland under control, and troops in the process of being evacuated from the islands.

At this point, differences of opinion between Rommel and Kesselring were

Mine-detection troops from the US 111th Engineer Battalion clearing the approach to Mount Lungo. The battles on the Winter Line would alter Allied strategy in Italy, switching the focus to Cassino and Anzio. (NARA via Digital History Archive)

exposed. While the former advocated a complete withdrawal to the northern Apennines in order to avoid the threat of an Allied landing behind the German defences, Kesselring thought that a prolonged defence of southern Italy was possible. As a matter of fact, both views had their pros and cons. Withdrawing north would spare Axis forces and reduce the threat of an Allied landing, while still controlling Italy's most important economic areas. On the other hand, maintaining control of southern Italy meant engaging the Allied forces, while at the same time exploiting almost the entire country and denying any political success to the Allied armies.

Hitler's concern was not with Italy. Focusing on a broader strategic view, he believed that leaving southern and central Italy to the Allies created a strategic vacuum which could permit a subsequent landing in the Balkans. Such a move, facilitated by the partisan operations in that theatre, would deprive Germany of important terrain and risk a link-up with the advancing Red Army on the Eastern Front, posing a major strategic threat to the Axis. Nevertheless, until mid-September, it was evident that Hitler had no clear idea about this theatre of war. In response to Kesselring's request, on 12 September Hitler informed him and Rommel that for the moment there would be no changes in command in Italy. Rommel could only issue orders to Kesselring once his withdrawing forces had reached northern Italy. Adhering to this order, two days later the Oberkommando der Wehrmacht (OKW, the Armed Forces High Command) ordered Kesselring to fall back to the Rome area no matter what. He was only asked to gain time in order to complete the evacuation of materiel and to complete the destruction of the lines of communication in southern and central Italy.

It is worth noting that, in spite of the situation (which saw 1.Fallschirmjäger-Division alone opposing the BR XIII Corps), Kesselring did not request reinforcements; and Rommel offered none. On 20 September, Kesselring defined AOK 10's task: it was to delay the Allied advance while preventing enemy landings on the Adriatic and Tyrrhenian coasts. While holding the Salerno line as a pivot, AOK 10 was to prepare a series of staged withdrawals to prepared lines. The first (Line O), running from Salerno to Manfredonia, was to be held until 30 September. The second (Line A, subsequently V or Viktor), running along the Volturno and Biferno rivers, would be followed by a third (Line A1, subsequently Barbara), running from Mondragone to Teano, Isernia, and the Trigno River.[2] Both lines had to be held until 15 October, gaining time to build the B (or Bernhardt) Line, running from the Garigliano River to Mignano, north of Isernia, Castel di Sangro and the Sangro River on the Adriatic coast. At the same time, Rommel ordered construction work to begin on the Gothic Line in the northern Apennines.

Bearing in mind a possible Allied threat to the Balkans, Hitler found Kesselring's idea of holding southern Italy appealing. The fact that only 11 divisions would be needed to hold the Bernhardt Line against the 13–20 needed to defend the Gothic Line surely helped. By 30 September, German strategy had already begun to change, and Kesselring was ordered to use delaying tactics up to the Gaeta–Ortona (or Bernhardt) line. The German thinking behind holding the line was thus: the Allies, having little interest in fighting a campaign in Italy, would switch to the Balkans, providing an opportunity for a German counter-attack in south-east Italy (Apulia).

2   The Germans frequently and repeatedly changed the names of these defensive lines; their latest designations are used here for simplicity.

However, Kesselring asked for six further divisions and a large contingent of air units to carry it out, and so this plan was eventually shelved.

More than anything else, the different attitudes of the two commanders influenced Hitler's final decision. Rommel showed great pessimism, an attitude made worse by his decision to withdraw (without Hitler's authorization) from El Alamein and by the subsequent withdrawal in northern Africa. Still the military idol of the German people, Rommel was losing prestige to the advantage of Kesselring, whose optimistic views on the future Italian campaign – irritating before the Italian surrender – were now offering more appeal and seemed possible. The two commanders expressed their views on 30 September in a conference with Hitler, who, on 4 October, maintained the status quo, ordering Kesselring to defend southern Italy while granting reinforcements from HGr B.

For about a month, until 6 November, Hitler remained uncertain about which strategy to adopt in Italy, in spite of an interview with Kesselring on 24 October. Without doubt, the slow pace of the Allied advance reassured him, and eventually contributed to his decision. On 6 November, Hitler decided to appoint Kesselring as commander-in-chief in Italy, with Rommel being appointed General Inspector of the Western Defences in North-West Europe. Most importantly, Kesselring was ordered to hold the Bernhardt Line, which was to mark the endpoint of the German withdrawal in Italy. His command, redesignated Oberbefehlshaber Südwest/Heeresgruppe C took over on 21 November as Rommel left Italy for France.

Facing the decision to abandon the Barbara Line, Kesselring and his staff decided to start preparing another defensive line partly matching the Bernhardt one, and partly intended to replace it in case of an Allied advance. The Gustav Line, which took its final shape in January 1944, followed the same outline as the Bernhardt Line along the Garigliano River, switching to Cassino and the Rapido River, and maintaining the same outline to Castel di Sangro. From there it moved to the east across the Maiella Mountains

Bodies of German soldiers about to be attended to by the American Red Cross. In spite of the severe losses suffered, the Germans were always able to maintain a degree of combat effectiveness thanks to reinforcements and replacements. (NARA via Digital History Archive)

massif down to the coast, across the line Guardiagrele–Lanciano–Ortona. Only in January 1944 did the Gustav Line adopt its final outline running from east of Guardiagrele to Francavilla a Mare, about halfway between Ortona and Pescara.

Because in late October and early November the eastern (Adriatic) part of the Bernhardt Line was seen as the most vulnerable to threats, the LXXVI.Panzer-Korps was reinforced and ordered to prepare defences in depth. This was also needed to create mobile reserves for use in any other threatened area, while holding the positions along the Sangro River, known to the Germans as the Siegfried Line or Advanced Bernhardt Line. Soon, the western (or Tyrrhenian) part of the Italian front became a cause for concern. Facing US Fifth Army's attacks, on 13 November AOK 10's commander General Joachim Lemelsen suggested a withdrawal to the east of the original Bernhardt Line at San Pietro Infine, leaving Mignano in American hands. Hitler took a personal interest in this matter, and the following day he ordered this position to be held and defended with the utmost vigour. This was in order to enable the construction of the Cassino position (eventually known as the Senger Line), which seemed a formidable position.

At a meeting on 15 November with Kesselring's chief of staff General Siegfried Westphal, Hitler assessed the situation in Italy. He agreed with his generals that the Bernhardt Line (and its future adjustments) represented the best and the shortest defensive line in Italy, which had to be defended to the last man. No further withdrawal was possible; the latest estimates suggested that no forces could be spared for a potential withdrawal to the Gothic Line. The final form of the Italian campaign had now taken shape.

THE CAMPAIGN

APPROACHING THE WINTER LINE

As Axis forces withdrew from Salerno on 17 September 1943, General Alexander ordered both the US Fifth and BR Eighth armies to advance at once. The next day, General Clark held a conference with his corps commanders, whom he ordered to advance towards Naples and east of Avellino. BR X Corps began its move along the coast, facing enemy delaying actions, and US VI Corps commenced its advance on 20 September, after General Lucas had taken over command. On 26 September, Clark requested the capture of Avellino, which was taken by US VI Corps on the 30th, two days after making contact with the withdrawing Axis forces. The BR X Corps, after facing a stubborn German defence on the 23rd, resumed its advance four days later and entered Naples on 1 October. The following week, Allied forces approached the Volturno River.

The advance of BR Eighth Army was even faster. Moving from Taranto, BR 1st Airborne Division passed Bari, making contact two days later with the CDN 1st Infantry Division advancing from Calabria. A giant leap was achieved as BR 78th Division landed one of its brigades (supported by Commandos) at Termoli on 2 October. Kesselring ordered an immediate counter-attack, involving 16.Panzer-Division. The division launched several attacks between 4 and 6 October, all without success. Eventually, the arrival of the bulk of BR 78th Division at Termoli on 7 October compelled Axis forces to withdraw. On 11 October, Foggia was seized, and having reached the line Termoli–Vinchiaturo, BR Eighth Army began to reorganize while Axis forces withdrew to the Trigno River.

The swift advance of Montgomery's army was probably behind Clark's decision to order BR X Corps across the Volturno without waiting for the US VI Corps, whose planned attack on 9 October failed because of heavy rains. In fact, both corps began their attacks on 13 October; the BR 46th Division faced German counter-attacks but managed to advance the next day, while the BR 56th Division followed across the Volturno and the BR 7th Armoured Division expanded its bridgehead.

To the east, the attacks by the US 3rd and 34th Infantry divisions also faced German counter-attacks, but the Americans succeeded in breaking the German defences. The following day, after the US 45th Infantry Division had seized Mount Acero, they began to move forward, securing US Fifth Army's eastern flank. With scarce forces to hand (15.Panzergrenadier-Division,

Mopping up the Mount Camino area, 12 December 1943. Corporal Carlyle W. MacLean kicks in a door while covered by Private A. Hamilton, both from BR 1st London Scottish Regiment. (NARA via Digital History Archive)

'Hermann Göring', 3.Panzergrenadier-Division and 26.Panzer-Division) and no prepared defences, von Vietinghoff authorized a withdrawal to the Barbara Line centred on Mondragone–Teano–Venafro and the Matese Mountains massif to the east. This was nothing more than a stopgap measure, since the Barbara Line had no prepared defences at all and mostly existed only on maps. The idea was to buy time to prepare the Bernhardt Line.

The US VI Corps rapidly increased the pace of its advance. With one infantry battalion fording the river, on 18 October the US 34th Infantry Division crossed the Volturno approaching Alife, which was secured on the 20th – the day after the US 45th Infantry Division had seized Piedimonte d'Alife. At this point the US 45th was pulled out of the front line and placed in reserve, leaving the US 34th Infantry Division to deal with German resistance for three days before resuming its advance on the 24th. Meanwhile, after also overcoming German resistance, the BR 46th Division resumed its advance on the 18th as the BR 56th Division moved towards Teano. On 24 October, the BR 46th Division switched east taking over BR 7th Armoured Division's positions, the move being completed on the 28th as the Germans withdrew. On the 30th, the BR 46th Division resumed its advance towards Sessa Aurunca, just as the BR 56th Division seized Teano. By 2 November, patrols from the BR 7th and 46th divisions had advanced as far as the southern bank of the Garigliano River.

Facing the Allied advance, XIV.Panzer-Korps had in fact abandoned the Barbara Line just as the US 34th Infantry Division approached the northern bend of the Volturno. Exploiting the moment, on the 29th, General Lucas reshuffled the US VI Corps with the US 34th and 45th Infantry divisions crossing the Volturno south of Venafro, while US 3rd Infantry Division was to advance towards Presenzano and Mignano. Beginning its move on 31 October, the US 3rd Infantry Division faced little German opposition and advanced towards the Mignano Gap, seizing the eastern slopes of Mount Sammucro, overlooking Route 6. Two days later, US 45th Infantry Division's crossing of the Volturno also encountered no opposition. The US 34th Infantry Division crossed the next day, overcoming obstacles and mines. On 4 November, the US 45th Infantry Division approached Venafro, while the US 504th PIR entered Isernia, linking up with BR Eighth Army. In 20 days the US Fifth Army had advanced between 25 and 36km along a 65km-wide front, without engaging the main body of the enemy forces. A pause was necessary, however, to rest and reorganize.

On 1 November, Kesselring issued orders stating that the Bernhardt Line had to be defended until the construction of the Gustav Line was completed. In a matter of days, the Allies resumed their advance on the eastern side of the front. Meanwhile, after reaching the Termoli–Larino area along the Biferno River, BR Eighth Army started regrouping. The BR 78th Division was deployed along the coast and the IND 8th Division inland; both were part

of BR V Corps. To the west of Foggia the CDN 1st Infantry Division acted as spearhead of BR XIII Corps, which in November also deployed the BR 5th Division. The regrouping was also necessary because BR Eighth Army, after facing only 1.Fallschirmjäger-Division, was now up against 16.Panzer-Division, 1.Fallschirmjäger-Division and 29.Panzergrenadier-Division, plus the incoming 65.Infanterie-Division.

Shortly after BR Eighth Army completed its regrouping on 22 October, having in the meantime cleared the approaches to the Trigno River, on the 24th, two Canadian brigades started advancing westwards after having seized Campobasso on 14 October. Facing little resistance, the CDN 1st Infantry Division crossed the upper Biferno River between 22 and 24 October, moving across the mountain roads north of Isernia. The town was seized on 4 November, linking both the US Fifth and BR Eighth armies and paving the way for the deployment of BR 5th Division. By 22 November, the BR 5th and CDN 1st Infantry divisions were nearing the upper Sangro to the south and north of Castel di Sangro, and had now encountered the Advanced Bernhardt Line positions.

On 27 October, the BR 78th Division established a small bridgehead on the Trigno, but the attempt to establish a second one that same night was repulsed by a counter-attack from the 16.Panzer-Division. Heavy rain meant that BR V Corps' planned attack had to be postponed from 29 October to 3 November, when the IND 8th Division crossed the Biferno followed by the BR 78th Division. The reaction of 16.Panzer-Division, concerned by possible Allied seaborne landings, was immediate, and a series of counter-attacks was unleashed before General Herr decided to withdraw to the Advanced Bernhardt Line. This made a steady advance by BR V Corps possible, with both its divisions able to approach the Sangro River by 9 November. By mid-November, as both armies paused to rest and regroup, the front line ran approximately from the Garigliano River to the Mignano–Venafro area, and from there to the Sangro River on the Adriatic coast.

US FIFTH ARMY PROBES THE WINTER LINE

The Mignano Gap, the valley across which both Route 6 and the Rome–Naples railway ran, was practically surrounded by mountains, which had to be taken in order to advance to Cassino and the Liri Valley. To the south, from east to west, three peaks dominated the area: Mount Camino, Mount La Difensa and Mount Maggiore. To the north, the wide-ranging Mount Sammucro formed, along with Mount Rotondo and Mount Lungo, a triangle with approximately at its centre the rural town of San Pietro Infine. Control of these heights would enable the Allies to reach San Vittore, and from there Cassino.

By November, it was already clear that seizing the mountains dominating the Mignano Gap would not be an easy task. From its positions north of Sessa Aurunca and Teano, BR X Corps moved on to attack Mount Camino with the BR 56th Division which, on 5 November, employed two infantry brigades in its assault. The next day, one of these was compelled to withdraw in the face of heavy resistance south of Mount Camino. A new attack was launched on the 7th, which once again encountered strong German counter-attacks over the course of the next two days. On 10 November, a peak to the immediate south of Mount Camino was secured, but had to be abandoned when the Germans counter-attacked. On 12 November, the entire BR 56th Division was committed, but with losses and exhaustion mounting, the planned attack was cancelled and, on 14–15 November the British troops were withdrawn from General Clark's chain of command.

On 5–6 November, the US 3rd Division sent its 30th RCT and one battalion of the US 15th RCT against Mount Rotondo and Mount Lungo. Attacking again on the 8th, the US 30th RCT took the summit of Mount Rotondo, while the US 15th RCT was halted on the slopes of Mount Lungo. On 5 November, the US 7th RCT attacked Mount La Difensa, facing the same obstacles as all the other attacking units: challenging terrain, a lack of roads, continuous enemy shelling, miserable weather and difficulties with supply. Only the US 45th Division, attacking on 6 November, enjoyed any success: it took height 1053 (Mount Corno, to the east of Mount Sammucro) and the nearby Mount Santa Croce. On the 10th, the US 1st Ranger Battalion took up position on the former, while a battalion from the US 504th PIR deployed on the latter. Just how precarious the American positions were was demonstrated on the 13th, when III./FJR 6 counter-attacked and managed to advance as far as the village of Ceppagna. This small but important town, dominating the road to San Pietro Infine, was retaken thanks to the intervention of the US 3rd Ranger Battalion.

On that same day, General Clark informed General Alexander that the frontal attacks against the enemy positions had exhausted his troops,

A patrol from K Company, 15th Infantry Regiment, US 3rd Infantry Division entering Mignano on 12 November 1943. The town's buildings had been destroyed by shelling from both sides of the front line. (NARA via Digital History Archive)

US Fifth Army's advance, October 1943 to January 1944

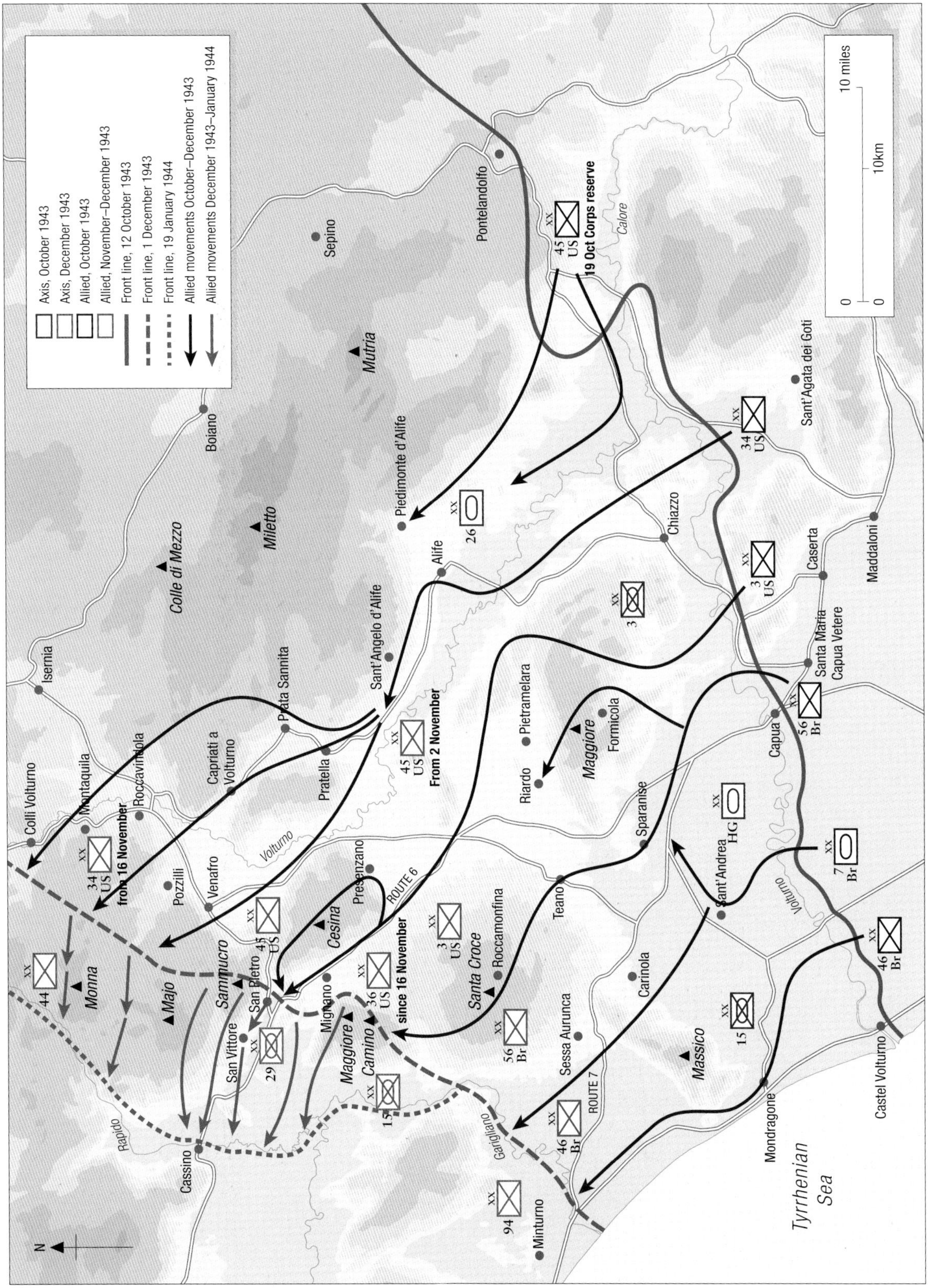

10 miles

10km

Calore

Pontelandolfo

45 US
19 Oct Corps reserve

34 US

Sant'Agata dei Goti

Sepino

Mutria

3 US

Caserta

Maddaloni

Piedimonte d'Alife

26

Alife

Chiazzo

3

Santa Maria
Capua Vetere

Boiano

Miletto

Sant'Angelo d'Alife

Prata Sannita

45 US
From 2 November

Pietramelara

Maggiore

Formicola

Capua

56 Br

Colle di Mezzo

Isernia

Capriati a Volturno

Pratella

Volturno

Riardo

Sant'Andrea
HG

7 Br

Montaquila
Roccavivola

Venafro

34 US
from 16 November

Pozzilli

Cesina

Presenzano

ROUTE 6

3 US
since 16 November

Roccamonfina

Santa Croce

Teano

Sparanise

Volturno

46 Br

Colli Volturno

44

Monna

Majo

Sammucro

San Pietro 45 US
San Vittore

Migano

36 US

Maggiore

Camino

29

15

Carinola

15

Massico

Rapido

Cassino

Sessa Aurunca

56 Br

ROUTE 7

Garigliano

46 Br

Mondragone

Castel Volturno

Tyrrhenian Sea

94

Minturno

N

in particular the US 34th, 3rd and 45th divisions, and suggested a halt. Alexander agreed, and two days later Clark paused US Fifth Army's advance in front of the Winter Line. A reorganization was started, with the US II Corps deploying in the Mignano area on 18 November with the US 36th Division in the line (from the 16th), and the US 3rd Division sent to the rear to rest and refit. The road from Ceppagna to San Pietro, between Mount Sammucro and Cannavinelle Hill, marked the boundary between the US II and VI corps, which deployed the US 45th Division in the southern area of its responsibility. Other units joined the US II Corps, including the US 1st SSF, a mixed American-Canadian formation deployed from 25 November, and the Italian co-belligerent 1° Raggruppamento Motorizzato (1st Motorized Group), a regimental-size unit. US Fifth Army also began to acquire mules and horses to bring supplies across the mountain tracks, only to discover there was a serious shortage of both. The creation of service companies by the Italian army proved of use.

Clark and his staff had a clear view of the situation, and considered the possibility of a Termoli-style seaborne landing behind German lines. However, the beaches in the Gulf of Gaeta, north of the Garigliano River, were deemed unsuitable, and other options to the north of the gulf were considered too far away for a rapid link-up. Somewhat surprisingly, a landing in the Anzio area was held under consideration. On the other hand, the US Fifth Army knew that it would take months before a full-scale offensive could be unleashed. The units of the Free French Corps would not be deployed until late December, the US 1st Armored Division arriving in Naples from 15 November to replace the BR 7th Armoured Division. Other reinforcements were long in coming: the US 88th Infantry Division was expected to arrive in Italy in February–March 1944, to be followed by the US 85th Infantry Division.

Even though they managed to hold the line, the situation for the Axis defenders was not much better. The 3.Panzergrenadier-Division, battered and heavily understrength, was relieved on 11–12 November by the 29.Panzergrenadier-Division, itself in poor shape having rested for just nine days. During a conference held on 8 November at the headquarters of XIV. Panzer-Korps, Kesselring and Lemelsen could only agree with General von Senger's observations. The defences of the Bernhardt Line at Mignano were wholly inadequate, and the available forces were insufficient to man them. The situation facing 3.Panzergrenadier-Division was revealing of the overall picture. Kesselring eventually released part of the reserves under his direct control, putting them under command of the XIV.Panzer-Korps, but was clearly reluctant to use the elements of the 'Hermann Göring' Division he still had available.

On the night of 11/12 November, 29.Panzergrenadier-Division's III./ Panzergrenadier-Regiment (PGR) 15 deployed on Mount Lungo, with I. and II./PGR 15 deploying to the north on Mount Sammucro. Also on the 12th, following a request to withdraw stragglers from San Pietro Infine to San Vittore, Kesselring commented that Hitler had given him and the local commanders a 'free hand concerning San Pietro' (*Countdown to Cassino*, p. 77). This was interpreted as authorization to withdraw from San Pietro, but news of this planned move provoked an immediate reaction from Hitler. San Pietro was to be held indefinitely, and in accordance with this directive II./PGR 15 was deployed there. When US Fifth Army halted its attacks three days later, it came as a much-needed relief.

General Clark's 24 November directives outlined a plan (entitled Operation *Raincoat*) that was formed by both the terrain and the forces available. The BR X Corps was to seize Mount Camino, while US II Corps was to take Mount La Difensa and Mount Maggiore. Afterwards, BR X Corps was to relieve US II Corps' units, freeing them up for the subsequent step: the seizure of Mount Sammucro and an advance along Route 6. The BR Eighth Army's offensive on the Adriatic coast would draw away some of the German reserves from the area. Clearly anxious to get a result, Clark moved forward the date of the planned attack, originally scheduled for 12 December.

American riflemen from an unidentified unit on the march in the Volturno area, in October 1943. The early stages of US Fifth Army's advance after the Salerno landings were characterized by comparatively rapid progress. (NARA via Digital History Archive)

The BR X Corps' attack began on 1 December, with BR 46th Division's diversionary attack being followed the next day by BR 56th Division's move on Mount Camino. The mountain summit was seized and then lost twice to German counter-attacks, British troops achieving final success on the 6th and declaring the Mount Camino area secure three days later. This matched US II Corps' plan, based on the US 1st SSF, in a daring move, seizing Mount La Difensa, and paving the way for the US 142nd RCT to take Mount Maggiore and the 141st RCT to attack Mount Lungo. The next and final step would be the seizure of San Pietro Infine.

The preliminary move against San Pietro began at 1630hrs on 2 December with a tremendous artillery barrage, 925 different artillery guns firing 75,000 high-explosive, phosphorous and smoke shells until darkness fell. For the first time, the 8in. artillery gun was used. After debussing at Presenzano, the men of US 1st SSF moved across unknown terrain through the US 142nd RCT lines. They advanced just as the barrage began, with I Company reaching the base of the northern cliffs at 2300hrs.

An M10 tank destroyer crosses the Volturno River via a pontoon bridge on 20 October 1943. American forces would cross the river three times, at different points. (NARA via Digital History Archive)

They began climbing at 0130hrs, dodging German machine-gun fire and struggling to carry their extra loads while ascending. At 0430hrs, the 2nd Regiment, US 1st SSF took the summit of Mount La Difensa in the face of German machine-gun and sniper fire. After a fierce struggle lasting for an hour, most of the German resistance was overcome. As the morning fog lifted, the 2nd Regiment probed forwards in the direction of Mount La Remetanea, overlooking Mount Maggiore.

At 0300hrs on 3 December, the US 142nd RCT's 2nd Battalion,

followed by its 3rd Battalion, started to advance north of Mount La Difensa, approaching Mount Maggiore at 1030hrs. Its summit was taken at 1700hrs and, as British troops advanced to Mount Camino and the Americans prepared a defence of Mount Maggiore, the III./PGR 129 began massing at Mount La Remetanea (between Mount Maggiore and Mount La Difensa) for a counter-attack. In view of the situation, General William Wilbur, US 36th Division's Assistant Commander, ordered the regimental reserves to deploy, while Colonel Robert Frederick, US 1st SSF's commander, asked for his unit to be relieved – which was practically impossible, given the terrain and the German artillery and mortar fire raining on Mount La Difensa.

The German counter-attack materialized in the night of 5/6 December against Mount Maggiore, held by 2nd Battalion, US 142nd RCT. On that same night, elements from the 1st and 2nd regiments, US 1st SSF commenced a two-pronged assault from the north and the south towards Mount La Remetanea, having repulsed the previous day a German counter-attack against hill 960. The summit was taken on 6 December, despite a German counter-attack, just as the British capture of Mount Camino signalled a German withdrawal. The last German assault was made on the 7th, once more against Mount Maggiore, but was halted by massive Allied artillery fire. The next day, the US 142nd RCT relieved the US 1st SSF, marking the end of Operation *Raincoat*.

The US 142nd RCT was relieved by the BR 56th Division in the Mount La Difensa–Mount Maggiore area on 10 December. This was a remarkable success, given that US 34th and 45th Infantry divisions had been attacking north of San Pietro since 29 November to distract the Germans, the former having advanced up to 4 December little more than a mile at a cost of 800 casualties. On 8 December, the US VI Corps' initiative all but ground to a halt as the US 34th Division was pulled back from the front, to be replaced by the FR 2nd Moroccan Division. Still, at the conclusion of *Raincoat*, only Mount Lungo and San Pietro Infine blocked the route to the Liri Valley.

THE FIRST BATTLE OF SAN PIETRO

Compared to the Mount La Difensa and Mount Maggiore areas, the San Pietro positions appeared relatively weak and easy to break through. The German defensive line was based on four key features: from the south, Mount Lungo, then the town of San Pietro and, to the north, two peaks that formed part of Mount Sammucro, heights 1205 and 950. While the approach route to Mount Lungo was clear, the approaches to Route 6 and San Pietro were rather difficult. The first comprised a deep gully running between Mount Lungo and Mount Rotondo, and the second ran across the southern slopes of Mount Sammucro with one track coming from Ceppagna, winding down to Cannavinelle Hill (Colle) and then rising again to reach San Pietro.

The US Fifth Army intelligence gathered on the German defences engendered a certain degree of optimism. On 29 November, the US 3rd Ranger Battalion carried out a probing attack towards San Pietro, only to provoke a German reaction that pinned it down and then compelled it to retreat. Another probe on 2 December faced no opposition. This led General Walker to assume the Germans were withdrawing, but thanks to patrols executed by the US 143rd RCT the situation in San Pietro was

San Pietro Infine, 7–18 December 1943

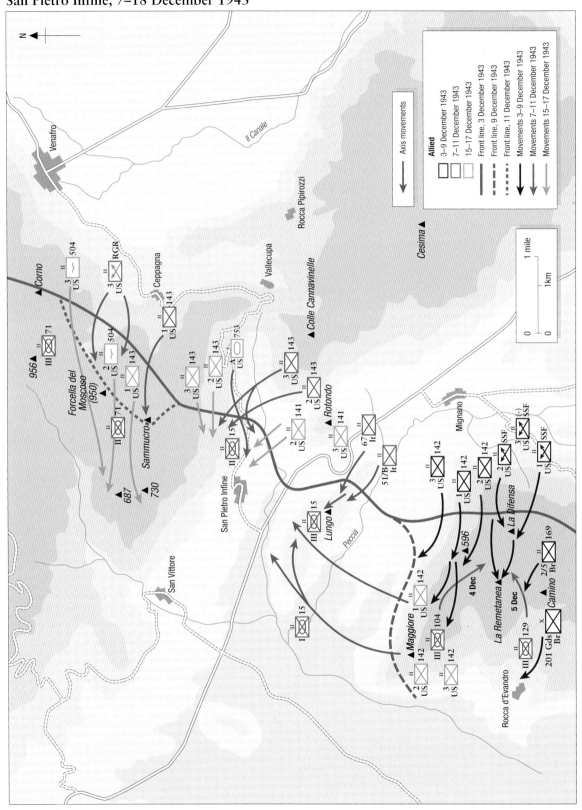

An improvised German pillbox on Mount Lungo. Made of stone and wood, it was covered with two layers of railroad ties. Von Vietinghoff complained about the poor quality of the Winter Line defences. (NARA via Digital History Archive)

reported accurately. There were plenty of German troops there, the town being heavily defended. In fact, II./PGR 15, some 400 strong, was deployed in the town. Less accurately, Mount Lungo was believed to be only lightly defended and easy to seize – in clear ignorance of the deployment in this area of III./PGR 15. To the north in the area defended by II./PGR 71, heights 1205 and 950 were not considered difficult obstacles to overcome. Such optimism led to a series of mistakes.

Eager to employ the co-belligerent Italian units on the battlefield, General Clark ordered the 1° Raggruppamento Motorizzato to seize Mount Lungo. The order did not take into account the actual condition of the Italian unit. Made up of a collection of hotchpotch units which escaped disarmament by the Germans, the 'Raggruppamento' (actually a reinforced regimental-sized unit) had amongst others two battalions from the 67° Reggimento Fanteria (infantry) which, as part of the 'Legnano' Division, had been used for garrison duties since 1941. The third battalion was a Bersaglieri (light infantry) one, and was an officer-training unit. Furthermore the Italian commander, clearly lacking experience, mistakenly assessed the artillery ammunition required, with the result that soon the Italian artillery was unable to provide support.

A further mistake was the dispersion of forces. Acting on Clark's input, General Keyes informed General Walker that a simultaneous attack on San Pietro, Mount Sammucro and Mount Lungo could lead to the collapse of the German defences, paving the way for an advance to Cassino. As a result, forces were scattered against a wide number of objectives, which turned

ALLIED ORDER OF BATTLE, SAN PIETRO

US 36th Infantry Division (Major-General Fred L. Walker)
36th Cavalry Reconnaissance Troop
111th Engineer Battalion
36th Divisional Artillery
155th Field Artillery Battalion
141st Regimental Combat Team (Lieutenant-Colonel Aaron A. Wyatt, Jr)
    1st–3rd battalions
131st Field Artillery Battalion
142nd Regimental Combat Team (Colonel George E. Lynch)
    1st–3rd battalions
132nd Field Artillery Battalion
143rd Regimental Combat Team (Colonel William H. Martin)
    1st–3rd battalions
133rd Field Artillery Battalion
Attached units:
636th Tank Destroyer Battalion

443rd AAA Automatic Weapons Battalion
753rd Tank Battalion (Lieutenant-Colonel Joseph T. Felber)
1st Special Service Force (Colonel Robert T. Frederick)
1st Regiment
    1st–2nd battalions
2nd Regiment
    1st–2nd battalions
3rd Regiment
    1st–2nd battalions
IT 1° Raggruppamento Motorizzato (Generale di Brigata Vincenzo Dapino)
67° Reggimento Fanteria
I, II and LI Battaglione Bersaglieri
504th Parachute Infantry Regiment (Lieutenant-Colonel Reuben Henry Tucker III)
    1st–3rd battalions
3rd Ranger Battalion (Major Herman Dammer)

out to be well defended. Nevertheless, Walker's plan was simple enough. Apart from the 1° Raggruppamento Motorizzato attacking Mount Lungo, to the north the US 3rd Ranger Battalion and the 1st Battalion, US 143rd RCT were to seize the key peaks of Mount Sammucro, heights 950 and 1205. In the centre, the 2nd Battalion, US 143rd RCT was to attack San Pietro, with the 3rd Battalion being held in reserve. Patrols were carried out to acquire knowledge of the area, while Allied artillery and medium bombers softened up the German defences.

A view of Mount Lungo, facing south, taken in December 1943. The photo shows, other than the mountain itself and the German emplacements, how all the trees and obstacles had been removed. The fields were then mined. (NARA via Digital History Archive)

After reaching their line of departure from Ceppagna, about an hour before dusk on 7 December the men of A Company, 1st Battalion, were briefed on the attack; they were to lead the battalion up to height 1205, with the other companies being held in reserve by the battalion commander. A Company started moving towards its objective at 1700hrs, and was surprised to discover that the path had not been mined and that there was no trace of German outposts. The summit was reached before dawn, and again German resistance was minimal, being soon overcome with grenades. Then the company dug in. Moving at the same time as A Company, the US 3rd Rangers Battalion approached height 905 faster than expected thanks to the easier terrain. By 0400hrs on the 8th, the Rangers had overrun German outposts about halfway to the summit, which was reached two hours later, despite German machine-gun fire hitting their rear positions.

It soon became clear that success would not come easy. Shortly after losing the two summits, at 0700hrs the Germans counter-attacked in strength. Height 1205 was almost lost at 0930hrs, when the Germans managed to advance thanks to a skilled use of cover provided by the terrain. A Company had lost one-third of its strength, and requested resupply and reinforcements. Only at this point did Burgess dispatch one platoon from C Company and another from the D Company, which succeeded in reaching the summit just in time to repulse the German attack. At 0830hrs, the German counter-attack hit the US 3rd Ranger Battalion at height 950, managing to bring fire on the summit from two positions. Unable to hold, the Rangers withdrew to the east, albeit reluctantly, reaching height 773. The Rangers reorganized and, after a preparatory bombardment by the US 131st Field Artillery Battalion launched at 0530hrs on 9 December, they reattacked height 950 and took it 30 minutes later. This was not the end of the matter: over the following four days, III./PGR 71 counter-attacked both heights 1205 and 950 several times, without success and paying a heavy price in losses. The opposing troops were also suffering; by 10 December, the 1st Battalion, US 143rd RCT was down to about 340 men, half its combat strength. In order to secure the area, on 12 December the US 504th PIR was brought into the line.

The seizure of heights 1205 and 950 seemed to pave the way for a breakthrough and to the fall of San Pietro Infine, but the illusion did not

A PAK 38 75mm anti-tank gun emplacement at Mount Lungo, destroyed by the Germans before their withdrawal. (NARA via Digital History Archive)

last long. Deployed on the line on 7 December, the 1° Raggruppamento Motorizzato did not carry out any reconnaissance of the terrain, nor did it send patrols. Preceded by artillery fire commencing at 0550hrs on 8 December, the Italians moved at 0630hrs from hill 253, the south-eastern slope of Mount Lungo, under cover of thick fog that acted like a smokescreen. It is worth noting, the Italian soldiers had been issued tropical uniforms for the simple reason that they were readily available in the Naples depots. Both the IT I./67° Reggimento Fanteria (on the right) and the IT LI Bersaglieri (on the left) battalions made little progress in the face of machine-gun fire emanating from the positions of III./PGR 15, which was well dug in. In spite of heavy casualties, by 1130hrs the Italians had halted and regrouped for another attack, this time supported by all of US II Corps' artillery. The second attempt was short lived, and by 1215hrs the Italians had withdrawn back to their starting positions deploying in defence of height 253.

Even though US II Corps' artillery prevented any German attempts to counter-attack, it was soon clear that the Italian efforts had ended in complete disaster. The 1°Raggruppamento was down to 700 out of its original 1,600 strength, most of the men (it is be believed) having simply deserted and fled the battlefield. The attack against San Pietro continued to paint the same picture. Moving from its positions on Cannavinelle Hill at 0700hrs on the 7th, the 2nd Battalion, US 143rd Infantry was supported at 0500hrs the next day by an artillery barrage. At 0620hrs, the battalion attacked towards San Pietro, and soon faced German fire. Heavy mortars, artillery and machine guns pounded the infantrymen who, after having advanced some 200m

AXIS ORDER OF BATTLE, SAN PIETRO

29.Panzergrenadier-Division (Generalleutnant Walter Fries)
Panzergrenadier-Regiment 15 (Major Georg Hufschmidt)
    I–III Bataillon
Panzergrenadier-Regiment 71 (Oberst Walter Krüger)
    I–III Bataillon
Artillerie-Regiment 29 (motorisiert) (Oberst Dr Fritz Polack)
    I–III Abteilung
Panzer-Abteilung 129
Panzer-Aufklärungs-Abteilung 129
Panzer-Pionier-Bataillon 29
Heeres-Flak-Abteilung 313
Nachrichten-Abteilung 29

15.Panzergrenadier-Division (Generalleutnant Eberhard Rodt)
Panzergrenadier-Regiment 104 (Oberst Karl Ens)
    I–III Bataillon
Panzergrenadier-Regiment 115 (Oberst Wolfgang Maucke)
    I–III Bataillon
Panzergrenadier-Regiment 129 (Oberst Albrecht Grell)
    I–III Bataillon
Panzer-Artillerie-Regiment 33 (Oberst Karl-Theodor Simon)
    I–III Abteilung
Panzer-Abteilung 215
Panzer-Aufklärungs-Abteilung 115
Panzerjäger-Abteilung 33
Panzer-Pionier-Bataillon 33
Heeres-Flak-Abteilung 315
Panzer-Nachrichten-Abteilung 33

from the line of departure, were halted by barbed-wire obstacles. Trying to cut the wire, the infantrymen discovered the wire was booby-trapped. Lieutenant Richard Stewart and several men from his platoon were killed when attempting to jump the barriers. The 3rd Battalion, US 143rd RCT was committed at this point, one of its companies advancing to the left of the 2nd Battalion, and two others to the right along the Ceppagna–San Pietro road.

A view of Mount Lungo from the west, with Mount Sammucro and San Pietro Infine to the left. Mount Maggiore is to the right. (NARA via Digital History Archive)

The former had to climb Mount Sammucro's slopes, only to discover that any clearing or gap was covered by enemy crossfire. In the words of a German soldier in San Pietro Infine, the defenders could cover nearly all the terrain to their front, which exposed any advancing enemy troops to their machine-gun fire. A German section, whose position had been spotted by the US infantrymen, was covered by accurate German fire that could shoot down anyone who attempted to assault the section's foxholes. Most importantly, the US infantrymen were not able to detect the positions of the German machine guns, firing at them from the flank. At nightfall the advance of both the 2nd and 3rd battalions, US 143rd RCT had been halted, and the artillery intervened with a barrage lasting through the night and into the early morning of 9 December. At 0700hrs that same day, the two battalions renewed their attack, which was characterized more by resignation than by enthusiasm. Once again, the German defences halted any attacking movement in spite of the heavy artillery support, enabling both battalions to achieve only insignificant gains.

With losses estimated at about 61 per cent of combat strength, no other options remained. At 1918hrs, the attack was called off, and the 2nd and 3rd battalions withdrew back to their starting positions. General Walker visited the men of the two battered battalions on 10 December, at last forming a clear picture of the situation. Meeting General Lucas two days later, Walker appeared deflated, which made Lucas wonder why, considering how little time his division had been employed at the front.

Men of US 36th 'Texas' Division approaching San Pietro Infine on 17 December along the narrow road which was used two days before for the failed tank attack. The wreck of a German truck and trailer can be seen. (NARA via Digital History Archive)

To make things worse, even though the US 36th Division's attack had ground to a halt on 10 December the Germans had no intention of sitting idle. Breaking the basic rule of counter-attacking during daylight, Oberst Krüger, commander of Panzergrenadier-Regiment 71, ordered Hauptmann Schneider, commander of the II.Bataillon, to make a night-time attack against height 1205. This began at 0045hrs on 11 December, two companies from II./PGR 71 attacking height 1205 and height 1142 (to the north-east); they managed to overrun the outposts of A

Company, US 143rd RCT, reaching the summits of the two heights. The American reaction came immediately with a heavy artillery barrage against the German troops, including the use of phosphorous grenades. This led Hauptmann Schneider to turn his attention at 0400hrs on height 950, but without success. After two hours of unsuccessful attacks and the pounding by artillery, the Germans eventually withdrew. Over the days that followed, any action was limited to artillery duels, harassing fire from one position against another, and the customary patrolling.

An 8in. howitzer from A Battery, US 194th Field Artillery Battalion firing at German positions on Mount Camino on 2 December 1943. This was the first time this weapon was used in combat. (NARA via Digital History Archive)

THE SECOND BATTLE OF SAN PIETRO

At the conclusion of the first attack against the town of San Pietro Infine, frustration prevailed. With both Mount Maggiore and Mount La Difensa seized to the south, and heights 1205 and 950 taken to the north, San Pietro was dominated from both sides – to little effect, however, since the Germans firmly held other key positions between those in Allied hands. These included Mount Lungo, protecting San Pietro from the south, and two points to the west of height 1205: hill 816, about 1.5km away, north of San Pietro, and farther to the west hill 730, dominating the town of San Vittore. Being to the west of San Pietro, along Route 6, it was the final prize. Farther to the north, forming a triangle on the western crest of Mount Sammucro, was hill 687. Clearly, as long as the Germans held those positions, San Pietro would be defended, making any further Allied advance impossible.

Unsurprisingly, General Walker's plan focused on the triangle on the western crest of Mount Sammucro. On 15 December, the 1st Battalion, US 143rd RCT was to move against heights 816 and 730, being supported in its action by the newly deployed US 504th PIR, which was to seize height 687 and send out patrols to the north in order to protect the right flank of the attack. There were no alternatives to using an already depleted battalion, given the lack of available units. Having belatedly realized that the Germans were determined to defend San Pietro, General Clark decided this was the target to seize and suggested that the next attack be supported by tanks. The suggestion did not convince General Walker, well aware of the difficulties of the terrain and of the inadequate lines of communication, but it seemed clear that if the chances of success of a tank attack were slim, the chances of yet another unsupported infantry attack were even slighter. For this reason, and persuaded by Clark's envoy Brigadier-General Donald Brann, Walker decided to give it a try.

In fact, the attack along Mount Sammucro's crest on its northern shoulder was the decisive one. Had those positions been taken, the Germans would have no longer been able to hold San Pietro Infine, or Mount Lungo. Still, and clearly with reluctance, Walker opted for a frontal attack against San Pietro in case the first one failed. This was to include the 2nd and 3rd battalions, US 143rd RCT moving against San Pietro north of the road from Ceppagna, and the 2nd Battalion, US 141st Infantry Regiment attacking from the south across the valley. Company A of the US 753rd Tank Battalion was to move along the Ceppagna–San Pietro road supporting the US 143rd RCT, itself supported by direct fire on San Pietro from B Company, US 753rd Tank Battalion and A Company, US 636th Tank Destroyer Battalion. These, firing from the northern slopes of Mount Rotondo, would hit targets in San Pietro and lay down a smokescreen to cover the tanks' advance. C Company, US 753rd Tank Battalion would be held in reserve.

Mount Lungo witnessed for the first time the employment of Italian troops fighting on the Allied side. This photo shows (from left to right) Lieutenant-Colonel Andrew F. Price, the artillery commander of the 1° Raggruppamento Motorizzato, Colonel Valfre Di Bonzo and Colonel Richard J. Werner. (NARA via Digital History Archive)

To complete the plan, the 1° Raggruppamento Motorizzato would attack Mount Lungo again, this time supported by the US 142nd RCT which, moving from Mount Maggiore, was to attack the eastern part of the mountain. If successful, the attack would clear the eastern crest of Mount Sammucro, San Pietro and Mount Lungo, paving the way for a successful advance towards San Vittore by the US 143rd RCT.

This would be a continuation of the previous attack, made by units already battered and worn out. Although not directly involved in the fighting, the US 504th PIR suffered 176 killed or wounded due to German artillery fire. The US 3rd Ranger Battalion also suffered heavily, with 35 killed and more than 200 men wounded or sick. US Fifth Army's commendation for the effort made during the first battle of San Pietro could not recover losses. The defenders were in no better shape. After six days of fighting, the 71.Panzergrenadier-Regiment reported the loss of 314 men, and 29.Panzergrenadier-Division's commander, General Fries, informed Kesselring that too much was being asked of his division. Kesselring replied that he should consider it a compliment. In truth, neither Kesselring nor Fries were in a position to do anything else.

American soldiers entering the ruins of San Pietro Infine on 17 December. (NARA via Digital History Archive)

On 14 December, the US Army photographic unit, commanded by Major John Huston (the famous Hollywood director), arrived at General Walker's headquarters. This was a consequence of General Clark's decision but, in spite of Huston's requests, Walker denied him permission to film the infantry and the tank attack, which he deemed to be dangerous. Most of the footage which would be shown in the famous

Troops from 3rd Battalion, US 141st Infantry Regiment return to the front line (after a mere two days of rest), moving along a railway track to avoid detection by the Germans, 12 December 1943. (NARA via Digital History Archive)

(and controversial) documentary *The Battle of San Pietro* would be filmed or re-staged at the end of the battle. Huston was not the only celebrity to document the battle, as the famous war correspondent Ernie Pyle also joined them at the divisional observation post.

The US 753rd Tank Battalion prepared thoroughly for the attack. The terrain was reconnoitred, spotting the elevation at the starting point (450m), which dropped to 220m at San Pietro Infine. The area leading to the town comprised terraces covered with olive trees and scrub vegetation, ranging from a height of 1–2m and a width of 3–6m. Most importantly, the terraces and the road were lined with rock walls, making detours off the main track possible only thanks to stream beds, gullies, cart tracks and accidents of the terrain. As the battalion's report made clear, 'a tank could not run from one terrace to the other in a westerly direction without engineer assistance' (*753rd Tank Battalion After Action Report*). From A Company's line of departure, set just after the road bent north-east of Cannavinelle Hill, the Shermans of US 753rd Tank Battalion had to deal with one small bridge, a large three-span bridge dominating access to the final track of the road, and then two culverts (one 10m wide, and the other, closer to San Pietro, 15m wide). To deal with these obstacles, a request was made to the BR X Corps for three Valentine bridgelayer tanks, but only one was delivered shortly before the attack; it was manned by a crew which had only a couple of days to acquaint themselves with the new vehicle.

Lieutenant-Colonel Joseph Felber, the US 753rd Battalion commander, carefully planned the attack. Once the main bridge had been crossed, the second platoon would detour from the main road and, using the trail running to the north-west, approach San Pietro via the terraces. The leading platoon would continue along the main road to another trail junction before splitting; one section, with the platoon leader, was to follow the trail and take position overlooking San Pietro to search for anti-tank guns. The second section was to proceed along the road to the town, blocking its exits. The third platoon would remain in reserve in the bridge area.

At 1100hrs on 15 December, Major George Fowler, A Company's commander, had the tanks moving along the road from their line of departure as the artillery shelled Monte Lungo with smoke grenades. Much to everybody's surprise, the three-span bridge was found intact, as was the ensuing culvert, making the Valentine tank redundant. Thus, it pulled off the road, making way for the others. At this point, Fowler ordered tank number No. 1 to detour on the trail, which was discovered to be impassable.

After breaking down part of the terrace wall, the tank made its way towards San Pietro. Again, much to the crew's surprise, the area was not mined. Tank No. 1 crawled its way towards San Pietro for about three hours crossing some 1,200m of open terrain, approached some buildings to the west destroying a machine-gun nest and a command post, then turned north, approaching San Pietro from the north-east. It did not face any anti-tank fire.

The others were not so lucky. Just after the culvert, tank No. 2 hit a mine and was blocked. Tanks nos. 3, 4 and 5 moved along the road, approaching San Pietro. As they reached the trail close to the town, they found it was blocked by a destroyed Panzer IV tank. Unable to proceed with the plan, the three tanks moved along the road and, as they approached the town's exit at 1511hrs, a German anti-tank gun opened fire. Tank No. 3 received a direct hit; tanks nos. 4 and 5 were also hit and set ablaze. The crews escaped, and surrendered.

Tank No. 2 from A Company, US 753rd Tank Battalion, which hit a mine shortly after the culvert and was immobilized during the 15 December tank attack. (NARA via Digital History Archive)

As it reached tank No. 2's position, tank No. 6 also hit a mine, as did tank No. 7, as it attempted to outmanoeuvre the others along the road. With the road basically blocked, tank No. 8 started pushing No. 7 out of the way, only to hit a mine itself. Unable to shift both tanks 7 and 8 off the road, tank No. 9 attempted to negotiate the wall on the right side of the road, getting struck in the process. As the smoke lifted, Major Fowler faced a difficult situation. German artillery started firing on the road and on the tanks; the road was practically blocked and only tank No. 1 gave good news. Major Fowler, in tank No. 10, decided to follow its path along with the remaining tanks, but, trying to negotiate the terrace on the path of tank No. 1, tank No. 12 turned on its side, blocking the way. As it tried to negotiate the terrace right behind it, tank No. 13 threw a track. At this point, Fowler ordered his tanks to turn back and try the other approach to the east, but while reversing onto the road, tank No. 11 slipped down the embankment and overturned. Fowler's tank, trying itself to get back onto the main road, accidentally hit tank No. 13, setting it back on its track. Fowler ordered it to provide covering fire against San Pietro.

Soldiers of the Italian 1° Raggruppamento Motorizzato bring back their wounded after the failed attack on Mount Lungo on 8 December 1943. The Italian performance was rather poor, with the unit suffering severe losses. (Keystone/Hulton Archive/Getty Images)

Eventually, Fowler managed to negotiate the terraces to the north-east of the road, followed by tanks nos. 14, 15 and 16. The first two threw their tracks, and were immobilized. Fowler's tank and tank No. 16 reached a ravine, blocking the way. As darkness approached, Fowler gave up and

A COMPANY, US 753RD TANK BATTALION ON THE ROAD TO SAN PIETRO INFINE, 15 DECEMBER 1943 (PP. 46–47)

By late afternoon on 15 December, it was clear that A Company, US 753rd Tank Battalion's attack against San Pietro was facing failure. The three tanks that, moving along the road, had reached the town had been destroyed by the Germans; all the others (apart from one, which made its way back) had been disabled by mines, or in their attempts to move along the road, or off it by negotiating the steep terraces to their right.

Close to the track leading to the terrace (**1**), tank No. 13 (**2**) was instructed by the platoon leader to move along the track and, while attempting to do so, it threw a track. It was the culmination of a series of unfortunate events, with tank No. 12 (**3**) overturning while negotiating the terrace, and, while moving along the main road, tank No. 11 (**4**) slipping off the road and falling into the embankment and overturning. Tank

No. 9 (**5**), farther down the road, had in the meantime become immobilized while attempting to negotiate the stone wall leading to the terrace. Luckily, tank No. 13 was accidentally hit by the company commander's tank, No. 10, as it backed up the road, which put tank No. 13 back on its track. The company commander then ordered tank No. 13 to remain in position and to provide cover fire against San Pietro during his attempt to outflank the town defences from the north along with tanks nos. 14, 15 and 16. The attempt failed, but tank No. 13 fulfilled its mission and was amongst the four Shermans (out of 16) that would make their way back to the starting line. Of the 12 Shermans disabled on the San Pietro Infine road, only five could be recovered after the Germans abandoned the town on 17 December.

ordered tank No. 1 to make its way back. Only four tanks out of 16 made their way back, the US 753rd Tank Battalion having suffered six men killed and eight wounded, one of whom died of his wounds. Eventually, 12 of the tanks were recovered after the battle was over.

Shortly after midnight the 1st Battalion, US 143rd RCT jumped off its starting positions, heading for height 730. The lack of vegetation meant the men were moving in the open, and soon they fell under German machine-gun and mortar fire. Once the base of the hill was reached, the infantrymen discovered that it was protected by a deep ravine. Unable to scale the height, the battalion took cover in the ravine, exchanging fire with the Germans. By 1000hrs, the battalion was down to a strength of 155, and short of ammunition. Supplies were brought in, but the US 504th PIR's attack also faced German resistance. About 500m before height 687, German machine guns brought its advance to a halt. The paratroopers had no other choice than to dig in on height 1205. At 1000hrs on 16 December, the II./PGR 71 attacked A Company's positions from two sides, without success. Eventually, 1st Battalion, US 141st RCT relieved the 1st Battalion, US 143rd RCT, which withdrew from its positions on 17 December.

At 1100hrs, the 2nd and 3rd battalions, US 143rd RCT started their attack to the north of the road leading to San Pietro Infine. Halted again by barbed wire and under direct German artillery fire, both battalions suffered heavy losses and were unable to advance. By the end of the day, E Company was down to seven riflemen, and had to be withdrawn. L Company, sent across the road to try and attack the town from the south-east, was halted as well in spite of reinforcements joining it at 1400hrs. By the end of the day the company was down to nine riflemen, and was forced to pull back as well. The entire 2nd Battalion was put in reserve, leaving in the area only the 3rd Battalion.

To the south, 2nd Battalion, US 141st RCT started its attack at 1253hrs from Mount Rotondo and soon faced German artillery fire. Any attempt to advance in what became known as the 'Valley of Death' proved impossible, and F Company switched its line of departure, moving now from a south-easterly direction. At 1730hrs, E Company led another attack, and also came under German fire. By 2000hrs, the battalion reported that its companies were down to an average of 52 men each. Communication having broken down, the battalion made another attempt. On the 16th, at 0100hrs, the 2nd Battalion attacked again, this time with some men actually reaching San Pietro and storming the German defences with grenades and bayonets fixed. However, as it reorganized at 0200hrs, the battalion was down to a total strength of 130, which did not prevent it from making a third effort at 0600hrs. A solid German defence made any further progress impossible, and at 1530hrs the remnants of 2nd Battalion were back at their line of departure.

Paratroopers from the US 504th PIR manning a .30-cal. light machine gun in the ruins of a house, 18 December 1943. This was the only American airborne unit to operate on the Italian front after the Salerno landings. (PhotoQuest/Getty Images)

Note: the base map covers an area of
approximately 4.5 x 3.5km (2.8 x 2.2 miles)

29 ⊠ xx

FRIES

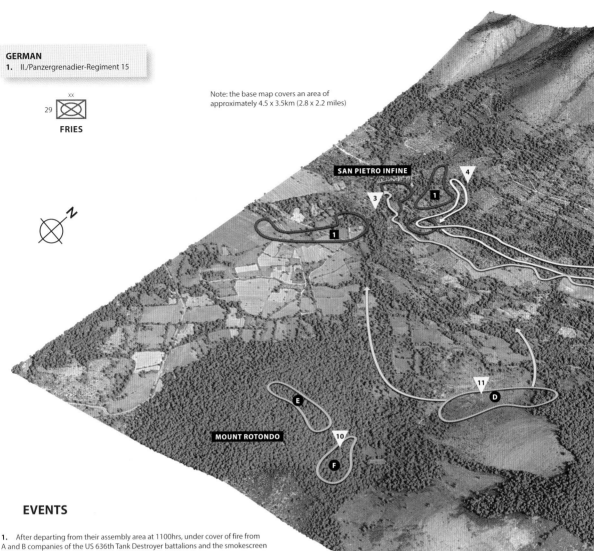

EVENTS

1. After departing from their assembly area at 1100hrs, under cover of fire from A and B companies of the US 636th Tank Destroyer battalions and the smokescreen laid by artillery, A Company moves along the road crossing the line of departure at noon. Finding the three-span bridge and the 3m culvert intact, the column advances towards San Pietro. Since the Valentine bridgelayer (tank No. 8) is no longer needed, it moves off-road making room for the column's advance. Tank No. 2, however, hits a mine and halts, while tanks nos. 3, 4 and 5 keep moving towards San Pietro.

2. In the attempt to attack San Pietro from two sides, the company commander orders his tanks to follow the track on the side of the road. Tank No. 1 complies with the order but soon abandons the track, advancing off-road. Tanks nos. 11, 12 and 13 are disabled while attempting to negotiate the track.

3. Tanks nos. 3, 4 and 5 approach San Pietro, trying to avoid a direct route. However, their attempt to move along a lateral road is rendered impossible by the wreck of a destroyed Panzer IV, which is blocking the way. The three tanks have no other choice than to approach San Pietro along the main road, and are destroyed one after another by German fire from the town.

4. After destroying a German machine-gun nest and a command post en route, tank No. 1 approaches San Pietro but, lacking support, it soon turns back and returns to the starting point, retracing its route.

5. Trying to bypass a tank blocked after hitting a mine, tanks nos. 6, 7 and 8 also hit mines and are immobilized. Tank No. 9 fails in its attempt to climb the terrace and is disabled.

6. Tank No. 10, with the company commander aboard, also fails in its attempt to negotiate the side track and, moving back, hits tank No. 13, fortuitously setting it back on its tracks. Then, tank No. 10 moves back along the road to join tanks nos.14, 15 and 16 for another attempt, ordering tank No. 13 to remain in place and provide covering fire.

7. Led by the company commander in tank No. 10, tanks nos. 14, 15 and 16 move off-road attempting another route of approach, but tank No. 10 is soon halted by a ravine; both tanks nos. 14 and 15 throw tracks, while eventually tank No. 16 is also disabled. By the end of the day, only four out of 16 tanks return to the starting positions.

8. At 1100hrs, E Company, US 143rd Infantry Regiment starts to advance towards San Pietro to support the tank attack. It is soon halted by barbed-wire obstacles and mines, the entire area being under German defensive fire. Reduced to seven riflemen by the end of the day, it pulls back.

9. L Company, US 143rd Infantry Regiment also advances towards San Pietro south of the road, and meets the same fate as E Company. In spite of reinforcements being brought in at 1400hrs to support the tank attack, L Company is reduced to nine riflemen by the end of the day and also pulls back. The 2nd Battalion, US 143rd Infantry Regiment goes into reserve and is replaced by the 3rd Battalion.

10. From the slopes of Mount Rotondo, both B Company, US 753rd Tank Battalion and A Company, US 636th Tank Destroyer Battalion support the attack with direct fire on San Pietro Infine.

11. Moving from their positions from the north-east of Mount Rotondo, at 1253hrs the 2nd Battalion, US 141st Infantry Regiment jumps off to attack San Pietro from the south. The German reaction is immediate, and the attacking companies fall under heavy artillery fire, which compels F Company to switch from the line of departure to the south-east. Facing the German fire from San Pietro, the attacking companies struggle to advance into what is soon dubbed the 'Valley of Death'. The attack is renewed at 1730hrs, with E Company in the lead, moving from the south-west end of Mount Rotondo. Once again, the German fire proves very effective and by the end of the day the 2nd Battalion companies are down to an average of 52 men each. A new attempt is made the next day, with a few men actually penetrating into San Pietro, but it is called off because of heavy losses.

ATTACK ON SAN PIETRO, 15 DECEMBER 1943

Following the failed attempt made on 11 December by 143rd Infantry Regiment, US 36th Division, on the 15th a combined tank and infantry attack was unleashed against the same objective. This time the US 143rd Regiment would be supported in its attack by 16 tanks from A Company, 753rd Tank Battalion, which would move against the town along the winding mountain road from Ceppagna. Terrain, and the German defences, meant the attack ended in disaster. Three tanks were destroyed by anti-tank fire, four others by mines and a further five would be disabled. Once again, the infantry, lacking tank support, were forced to withdraw before reaching San Pietro.

MOUNT SAMMUCRO

CANNAVINELLE HILL

US 36   WALKER

US
A. A Company, US 753rd Tank Battalion
B. E Company, US 143rd Infantry Regiment
C. L Company, US 143rd Infantry Regiment
D. 2nd Battalion, US 141st Infantry Regiment
E. B Company, US 753rd Tank Battalion
F. A Company, US 636th Tank Destroyer Battalion

The inhabitants of San Pietro Infine took shelter during the battle in nearby caves. Here, an Italian woman is kissing the hand of Colonel William H. Martin, commanding officer of US 143rd Infantry Regiment, after his arrival in the town on 17 December 1943. (NARA via Digital History Archive)

Success came from an unexpected direction. At 1730hrs on the 15th, the 3rd Battalion, US 142nd RCT attacked the northern end of Mount Lungo and, thanks in part to the courage of 2nd Lieutenant Joseph W. Gill, was able to silence 15 German positions (the area was defended by Aufklärungs-Abteilung 129). Meanwhile, snipers took out other machine-gun nests. By dawn on the 16th, the summit of Mount Lungo had been cleared and was firmly in the hands of the men of US 36th Division. The 1st Battalion, US 142nd RCT followed suit and that same day secured the central areas of the mountain. Even the Italian attack, which started at 0915hrs, was successful, and by the early afternoon the 1° Raggruppamento Motorizzato had taken the southern portion of Mount Lungo.

A counter-attack against Mount Lungo and a storm of artillery fire came from the German side in the afternoon of 16 December. It was in fact a feint, aimed at covering the German withdrawal. The reasons for this move were clear. By seizing Mount Lungo, the US 36th Division was now able to overlook San Pietro Infine and its approaches, an advantage that could be increased further if another attack on Mount Sammucro succeeded in seizing heights 730 and 687. Withdrawal was the only possible option, and on 17 December US 36th Division's troops entered what remained of San Pietro Infine – a town completely destroyed, and no longer worth rebuilding. This success was only limited, though. Soon the US troops discovered that a new German defensive line had been built only a few hundred metres away, barring access to San Vittore.

On 19 December, the US 3rd Division had its 15th RCT relieve the US 142nd RCT on Mount Lungo, before itself being replaced by the US 34th Division at the end of the month. In December, the US 36th Division lost a total of 1,772 men, 1,200 of whom became casualties during the San Pietro battles. The total included approximately 150 killed in action, 800 wounded and 250 missing. The US 504th PIR alone lost 50 killed, 225 wounded and two missing. The 29.Panzergrenadier-Division was relieved on 31 December by 44.Infanterie-Division. There are no details of its losses, which certainly matched – if not surpassed – those of US 36th Division.

BR EIGHTH ARMY'S CROSSING OF THE SANGRO

With his forces approaching the Sangro River since 9 November, General Montgomery prepared for the next step of the offensive. Since only the coastal road was suitable for large-scale action, his plan focused on the BR V Corps which, with the BR 78th and the IND 8th divisions, was to attack on a narrow front about 8km wide on the coast. The attack was to be supported

BR Eighth Army's advance, November 1943–January 1944

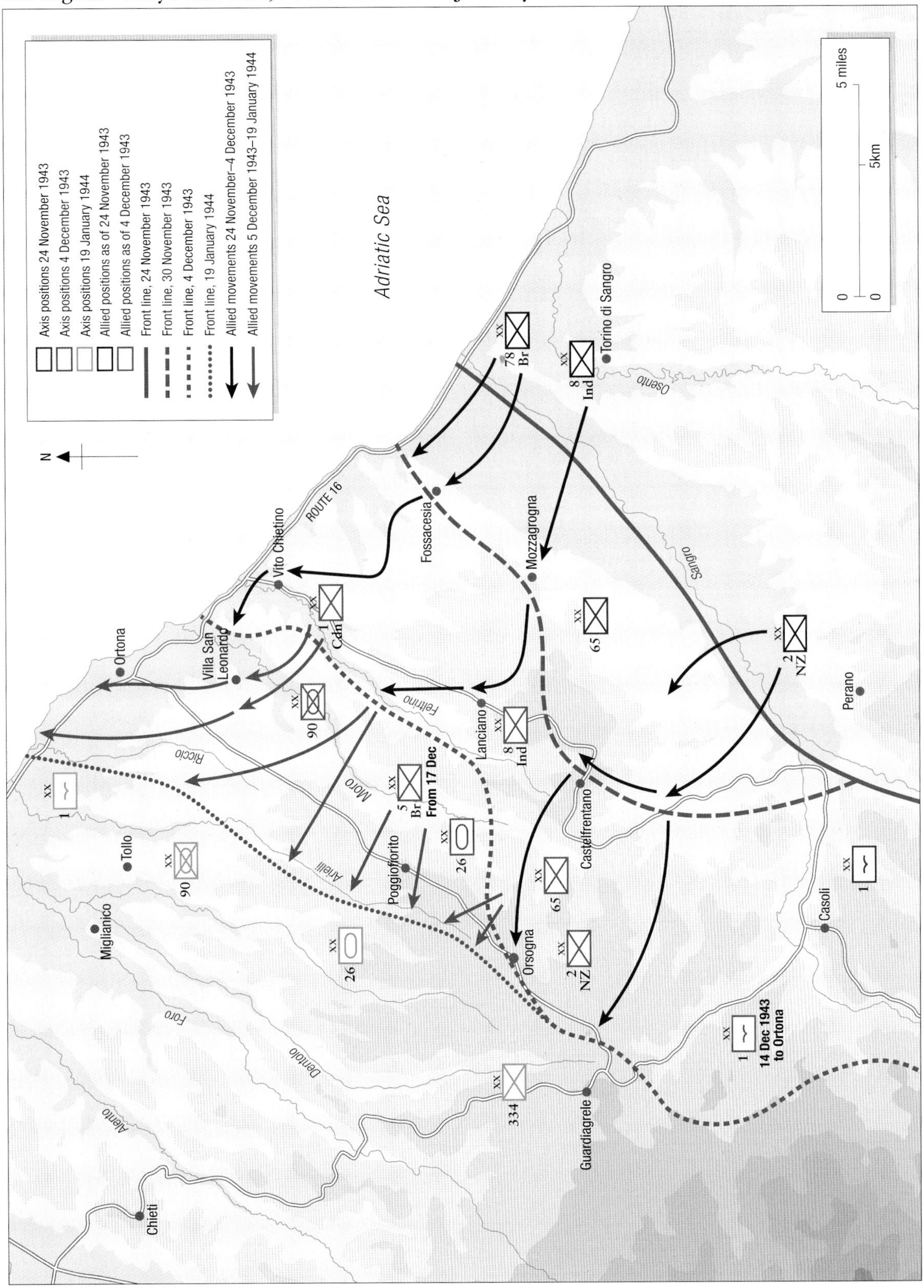

Legend

Axis positions 24 November 1943
Axis positions 4 December 1943
Axis positions 19 January 1944
Allied positions as of 24 November 1943
Allied positions as of 4 December 1943
Front line, 24 November 1943
Front line, 30 November 1943
Front line, 4 December 1943
Front line, 19 January 1944
Allied movements 24 November–4 December 1943
Allied movements 5 December 1943–19 January 1944

N

5 miles

5km

Adriatic Sea

Torino di Sangro

Osento

Sangro

Perano

78 Br

8 Ind

ROUTE 16

Vito Chietino

Fossacesia

Mozzagrogna

65

2 NZ

Ortona

1 Cdn

Villa San Leonardo

Feltrino

Lanciano

8 Ind

Castelfrentano

Riccio

90

Moro

5 Br
From 17 Dec

26

Casoli

1

Tollo

90

Arielli

Poggiofiorito

Orsogna

2 NZ

65

Miglianico

26

14 Dec 1943
to Ortona

1

Foro

Dentolo

334

Guardiagrele

Alento

Chieti

53

A scout car crew of the 6th Duke of Connaught's Own Lancers, Indian Armoured Corps, chats with youngsters during the advance towards the Sangro in early November 1943. (Photo by Sgt. Rooke/ Imperial War Museums via Getty Images)

by the NZ 2nd Division, moving on the left flank towards Guardiagrele and aiming to reach Chieti. The BR XIII Corps was to continue its advance on the upper Sangro in the Alfedena–Castel di Sangro area, to deceive the Germans. These plans did not take into account the pouring rain, which turned out to be the major hurdle.

From 10 November, patrols from BR 78th Division, including engineers and anti-tank elements, had crossed the Sangro without opposition. Five days later, the rain made any fording practically impossible. On 22 November, the division carried out a major crossing, with BR 11th and 36th brigades establishing a bridgehead about 2km deep and 5km long, just in front of the Bernhardt Line defences. Meanwhile, the NZ 2nd Division approached the river, taking Perano on the 19th. The Sangro was secured within a few days, with BR 78th Division's engineers laying bridges across the river from 21–22 November, despite its swollen status. Three days after the planned deadline, on 27 November the IND 17th Infantry Brigade and the BR 38th Infantry Brigade crossed the Sangro heading for Mozzagrogna. After a fierce struggle for control of the town with 65.Infanterie-Division's 145.Infanterie-Regiment, at dawn on the 28th elements from II./Panzer-Regiment 26 counter-attacked, driving the Indian and British forces away. This setback proved to be temporary for, at the same time, BR 4th Armoured Brigade was crossing the river. On the 29th, the Indians retook Mozzagrogna, clearing the way for BR 78th Division's assault. Meanwhile, the NZ 2nd Division had crossed the Sangro to the south the previous day, heading for Sant'Eusanio and Castelfrentano. With II./GR 145 practically wiped out and Panzergrenadier-Regiment 67 unable to reach the front because of air attacks, there was little the Germans could do.

During the night of 29/30 November, the BR 78th Division, supported by tanks, outflanked the Bernhardt Line position moving from Mozzagrogna to Fossacesia, then advanced north to seize Rocca on 1 December. Also on 30 November, the NZ 2nd Division approached Castelfrentano, before turning westwards. That same day, two battalions of Panzergrenadier-Regiment 67 reached Arielli, where a mobile force was to be assembled along with elements from 90.Panzergrenadier-Division's Panzergrenadier-Regiment 361 and II./Panzer-Regiment 26. As they gathered, the enemy threat from Rocca and Castelfrentano made any counter-attack impossible. The LXXVI.Panzer-Korps's commander, General Herr, opted to delay the enemy on the Feltrino River along the line San Vito Chietino–Lanciano–Castelfrentano, while preparing a defensive line running from Ortona to Orsogna and Guardiagrele – the so-called 'Siegfried Line'. The depleted German forces could not prevent BR Eighth Army from breaking through the eastern portion of the Bernhardt Line, let alone counter-attack at all. On 2 December, as the NZ 2nd Division moved towards Orsogna and Melone, the IND 8th Division approached Lanciano, which was taken the next day. Given the lack of forces and BR V Corps's advance, General Herr had by now already ordered a major withdrawal to the Siegfried Line.

On 3–4 December, the BR 78th Division advanced along the coast breaking through the German defences and seizing San Vito, even before BR 38th Brigade approached the Moro River. The brigade was temporarily under the command of the CDN 1st Infantry Division, which on 2 December began to relieve the BR 78th Division. In two days, the Canadians deployed along the Moro, with orders to cross it as soon as possible. The IND 8th Division was to support the left wing of the Canadian advance, which it did outflanking the Feltrino River with a steady advance that brought the Indian units to the Moro two days later. In the meantime, the battle for Orsogna had already begun.

An Allied Sherman tank advances towards the Sangro River, with the Maiella Mountains in the background, in November 1943. (Public domain)

NZ 2ND DIVISION'S FIRST ATTEMPTS AGAINST ORSOGNA

The New Zealanders' advance from the bridgehead on the Sangro started on 29 November, with the NZ 24th Battalion on the left (western) flank, the NZ 25th and 26th battalions in the centre and the NZ 21st and 23rd battalions on the right (eastern) flank. By the next day, the units had reached a line running from the Sant'Eusanio railway station (east of the town) to a ridge less than 2km away from Castelfrentano. The NZ 24th Battalion, redeployed in the centre, advanced to within 500m of the town. The depleted German units, unable to halt the enemy advance, had no choice but to withdraw. On 1–2 December, III./GR 146 abandoned Castelfrentano to redeploy, together with II./GR 146, along the Orsogna–Ortona road. The withdrawal of II./FJR 1 was slower, the unit moving towards Orsogna in order to enable Aufklärungs-Abteilung 26 to deploy in the town by the end of 2 December, securing the western tip of the Siegfried Line.

The German withdrawal caught the New Zealanders by surprise, which, coupled with the rugged terrain and lacking communications, did not permit any breakthrough or exploitation. After seizing Castelfrentano, the NZ 24th Battalion advanced north to the Brecciarola Ridge and the old Roman road, running east from Orsogna. The NZ 25th Battalion, slowed by the Fallschirmjäger and the terrain, merely approached the southern ridge of Orsogna, the Chiamato Hill, with the bulk of the battalion moving north towards Frisa. Here, on the eastern flank, the situation was better with the NZ 23rd, 26th and 28th battalions deploying around Castelfrentano before advancing towards Lanciano.

The Battle for Orsogna, 1–25 December 1943

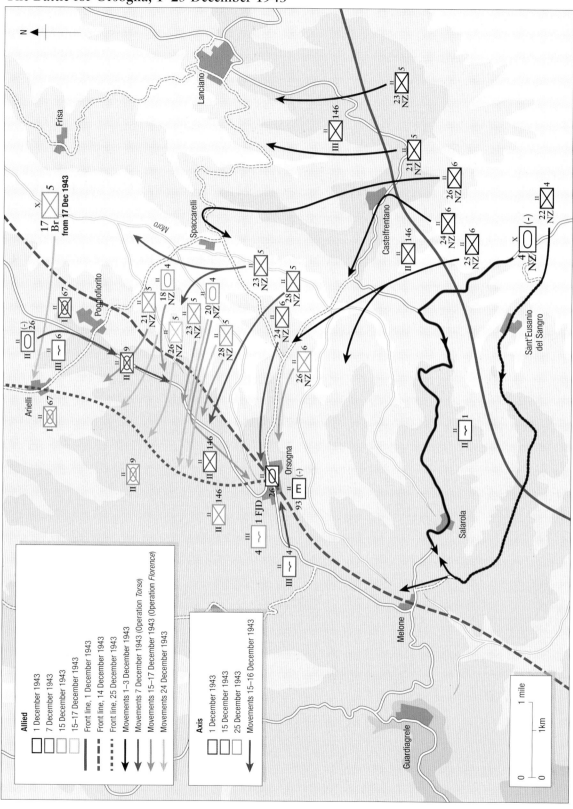

The only real attempt to break through the German lines was made on 2 December by the NZ 4th Armoured Brigade, on the western flank of the division. Moving from Sant'Eusanio railway station, B Squadron of NZ 18th Armoured Regiment supported by the 2nd and 3rd companies from NZ 22nd Battalion approached Salarola from the north using the Castelfrentano–Salarola road. The C Squadron, NZ 18th Armoured Regiment and NZ 22nd Battalion's 1st Company were to advance from the south, along the Sant'Eusanio–Salarola road, both led by the armoured cars of the divisional Cavalry Regiment. Soon after departure, the first column encountered an obstacle north of the station, but managed to reach the road junction to Salarola only to be fired upon by German artillery. The Germans, comprising a platoon from I./PGR 9 supported by two Panzer IVs, attempted to halt the New Zealander column but without success. One Panzer IV was destroyed and the *Panzergrenadiere* withdrew, enabling the column to reach Salarola. Any further advance was made impossible by artillery fire and demolition obstacles, and only a patrol from 2nd Company managed to move past the road junction towards Melone, before soon being compelled to withdraw.

Fallschirmjäger on the march in Italy. Until the Termoli landings, 1.Fallschirmjäger-Division was the only German unit deployed along the Adriatic coast opposing the advance of BR Eighth Army. (Narodowe Archiwum Cyfrowe)

The southern column, delayed by German machine-gun nests and demolition obstacles, managed to reach the junction at night linking up with the northern column. At 0800hrs on 3 December, the 2nd and 3rd companies, NZ 18th Battalion and B Squadron, NZ 18th Regiment attacked Melone, which was defended by elements of II./FJR 1. Facing German heavy artillery fire, the New Zealanders were unable to dislodge the defenders, and only succeeded in taking refuge in some houses on the outskirts of the town. Other attempts were made on 4 and 5 December, without success, and eventually the plans to advance towards Guardiagrele were cancelled. Between 6 and 7 December, the NZ 4th Brigade's 22nd Battalion was relieved in the area by elements from BR 2nd Parachute Brigade.

ALLIED ORDER OF BATTLE, ORSOGNA

NZ 2nd Division (Lieutenant-General Sir Bernard Freyberg)
NZ 4th Armoured Brigade (Brigadier Keith L. Stewart)
    NZ 18th Armoured Regiment
    NZ 19th Armoured Regiment
    NZ 20th Armoured Regiment
    NZ 22nd Motor Battalion
NZ 5th Brigade (Brigadier Howard K. Kippenberger)
    NZ 21st New Zealand Battalion
    NZ 23rd Battalion
    NZ 28th (Maori) Battalion
NZ 6th Brigade (Brigadier Graham B. Parkinson)
    NZ 24th Battalion

NZ 25th Battalion
NZ 26th Battalion
Divisional artillery
    4th Field Artillery Regiment
    5th Field Artillery Regiment
    6th Field Artillery Regiment
    7th Anti-tank Regiment
    14th Light Anti-Aircraft Regiment
Divisional Cavalry Regiment (reconnaissance)
NZ 27th (Machine-Gun) Battalion
5th–8th Field companies engineers

Over these days, the New Zealanders were to discover how determined the Germans were to defend this area. Ordered to attack Orsogna in the morning of 3 December by Brigadier Graham Parkinson, the NZ 25th Battalion, deployed about 1.5km to the east along the old Roman road, probably expected yet another German withdrawal. While the road was reconnoitred and improved for use by tanks, in the early hours the battalion advanced without problems. At 0315hrs, Lieutenant-Colonel T.B. Morten, the battalion commander, deployed A Company about 1km east of the town, which was approached by C and D companies. Once in the town, the former company took up positions at its entrance while the latter entered Orsogna, reaching its main square and deploying three platoons. Attacked by one of Aufklärungs-Abteilung 26's AFVs, the New Zealanders scattered, seeking cover in the buildings in the southern part of the town. At 0800hrs, 2. and 4.Kompanie, Aufklärungs-Abteilung 26 supported by five panzers from 6.Kompanie, II./Panzer-Abteilung 26 counter-attacked from the west, cutting off the two platoons. Allied artillery support proved useless, with shells actually hitting the houses in which the New Zealanders were hiding.

The German counter-attack led to A Squadron, NZ 18th Tank Regiment (deployed some 13km away) being moved up. As its Shermans approached Orsogna, they were halted by the German armour; A Squadron only succeeded in damaging a Panzer IV before withdrawing. The belated tank attack merely succeeded in enabling the men of D Company to withdraw. The 16th Platoon, in particular, remained behind to cover the withdrawal, and only seven men managed to escape along a trail in the southern part of the town. By 1100hrs, the New Zealanders' withdrawal was complete, the NZ 25th Battalion having lost four killed, 26 wounded and 53 missing, mostly taken prisoner. A concerted effort would be needed to take Orsogna.

AXIS ORDER OF BATTLE, ORSOGNA (AND ORTONA)

26.Panzer-Division (Generalleutnant Smilo von Lüttwitz)
Panzergrenadier-Regiment 9 (Oberstleutnant Oskar-Alfred Berger)
    I–II Bataillon
Panzergrenadier-Regiment 67 (Oberst Horst von Usedom)
    I–II Bataillon
Panzer-Regiment 26 (Oberst Johannes Kümmel)
    I–II Abteilung
Panzer-Artillerie-Regiment 93 (Oberst Wilhelm Viebig)
    I–III Abteilung
Panzer-Aufklärungs-Abteilung 26
Panzer-Pionier-Bataillon 93
Heeres-Flak-Artillerie-Abteilung 304
Panzer-Nachrichten-Abteilung 93
65.Infanterie-Division (Generalmajor Gustav Heistermann von Ziehlberg, from 1 December Generalmajor Hellmuth Pfeifer)
Grenadier-Regiment 145 (Oberst Hans-Wilhelm Krökel to 5 December, then Oberst Claus Kühl)
    I–III Bataillon
Grenadier-Regiment 146 (Oberst Martin Strahammer)
    I–III Bataillon
Artillerie-Regiment 165 (Oberst Gustav Körner)
    I–III Abteilung
Aufklärungs-Abteilung 165
Panzerjäger-Abteilung 165
Pionier-Bataillon 165
Nachrichten-Abteilung 165
1.Fallschirmjäger-Division (Generalleutnant Richard Heidrich)
Fallschirmjäger-Regiment 1 (Major Wolf-Werner von der Schulenburg)
    I–III Bataillon
Fallschirmjäger-Regiment 3 (Oberst Ludwig Heilmann)
    I–III Bataillon
Fallschirmjäger-Regiment 4 (Major Reinhard Egger)
    I–III Bataillon
Fallschirm-Artillerie-Regiment 1 (Oberst Bruno Schram)
    I–III Abteilung
Fallschirm-Panzerjäger-Abteilung 1
Fallschirm-Pionier-Bataillon 1
Fallschirm-Nachrichten-Abteilung 1

THE BATTLE OF ORSOGNA: OPERATION *TORSO*

Clearly, a head-on assault against the German positions had become impossible in early December. Having abandoned any attempt to move against Guardiagrele, given the unsuitable terrain, Orsogna became the cornerstone of the New Zealanders' attempts to pierce the German defences. The plan of Operation *Torso* took these factors into account. After redeployment, the NZ 2nd Division was to attack with the NZ 5th Brigade (23rd and 28th battalions) north of Orsogna moving across the Pascuccio and Sfasciata ridges to reach the Orsogna–Arielli road. While the NZ 5th Brigade covered the second part of the pincer paving the way for an attack from the north, the NZ 6th Brigade (24th Battalion), supported again by the NZ 18th Armoured Regiment, was to attack along the Roman road.

A soldier from the NZ 2nd Division looks towards Orsogna on 7 December. (© Imperial War Museum, NA 9706)

H-hour was set for 1330hrs on 7 December. The artillery opened fire, but clouds prevented effective air support. Also, the NZ 23rd Battalion jumped off without any previous reconnaissance, having reached the starting line late. Nevertheless, well protected by mortar fire from the NZ 27th Battalion and facing no opposition, it crossed the Sfasciata Ridge and deployed at 1510hrs to defend the northern flank of the attack. At 1430hrs, the NZ 28th (Maori) Battalion moved across Pascuccio Ridge, soon facing German resistance and a minefield. C Company, led by Captain Wirepa, overcame it and at 1700hrs reached its target: the Orsogna–Arielli road on the battalion's right flank. D Company, led by Captain Ornberg, also faced German resistance but, supported by C Company, eventually deployed along the road to the north of the cemetery. A Company, led by Captain Henare (B Company remained in reserve), managed to outflank two platoons of 7.Kompanie, II./PGR 9 which, attacked from the rear, were overcome. This enabled A Company to deal successfully with the positions held by II./GR 146 and reach its positions to the south of the cemetery, deploying between the road and the railway.

Looking towards Orsogna from Allied positions approaching the town. (© Imperial War Museum, NA 9604)

Preceded by an air attack against Orsogna, at 1410hrs the NZ 24th Battalion jumped off from its starting position, advancing along the Roman road. At 1600hrs, A Company, supported by A Squadron, NZ 18th Armoured Regiment, passed some demolition obstacles only to be halted some 150m from the town gate by a Panzer IV firing on the New Zealander

PANZER-REGIMENT 26 HALTS THE NZ 24TH BATTALION ADVANCE ON ORSOGNA, 7 DECEMBER 1943 (PP. 60–61)

After the NZ 25th Battalion's failed attempt to seize Orsogna on 2–3 December, on 7 December A Company, NZ 18th Armoured Regiment made another attempt to do so. The plan of Operation *Torso* comprised a two-pronged attack on Orsogna, with the NZ 6th Brigade attacking frontally along the old Roman road, an unpaved track leading directly to the centre of the town, and the NZ 5th Brigade attacking to the north moving across the Spaccarelli Ridge. The NZ 4th Brigade, the armoured element of NZ 2nd Division, was to support NZ 6th Brigade's attack with the 18th Regiment and, where possible, the NZ 5th Brigade with the tanks of 20th Regiment.

Since the latter proved unable to cross the rugged terrain, A Company, NZ 18th Armoured Regiment would be the only armoured unit to face the German defences. Supporting the NZ 24th Battalion's advance, and with the help of divisional sappers, A Company moved along the old Roman road overcoming obstructions and a first German tank, which was forced to pull back. A second one was destroyed but, approaching about 150m from Orsogna's entrance gateway, the Shermans (**1**) were halted by a crater in the road, and by a Panzer IV tank (**2**) reinforced on both sides by machine-gun nests located in the ruins of the houses. Any attempt to approach the houses was made vain by the German machine-gun fire, by the tank also firing its gun, and by the crater in the road which the sappers were unable to fill. After unsuccessful attempts, and given the withdrawal of NZ 5th Brigade units, the men of NZ 24th Battalion and the tanks of A Company had no other choice than withdrawal under the cover of darkness. The second attempt to seize Orsogna began once again with failure for the NZ 18th Armoured Regiment.

infantry and Sherman, its flanks protected by machine-gun nests hidden in the nearby houses. The tanks were unable to move forward since a large crater, which had been mined, blocked the way and the supporting engineers, with two bulldozers, could not overcome the obstacle. The men of A Company deployed on both sides of the road, its headquarters was installed in the nearby 'Pink House'.

Taking advantage of the gully to the south of the town, B Company saw its 10th and 11th platoons eventually enter Orsogna at 2100hrs, just as C Company's 13th Platoon did the same from the north. The other platoons were deployed on the town's southern and northern approaches, but were unable to move forward because of the German machine-gun fire. The men of Aufklärungs-Abteilung 26 (supported by 3.Kompanie, Pionier-Bataillon 93) counter-attacked, supported by the tanks of II./Panzer-Regiment 26 (which also included a Flammenwerfer Panzer III from the regimental flamethrower company), and the New Zealanders' requests for reinforcements were eventually answered with a withdrawal order. In fact, after midnight, the 10th Platoon managed to escape the town by hiding in a cave, while the remnants of the others withdrew and joined the rest of the battalion.

Bombs exploding in Orsogna after a first softening-up attack by Allied Kittyhawks on 8 December. The Kittyhawks each carried one heavy bomb. (© IWM NA 9602)

In the meantime, D Company, NZ 28th Battalion was attacked in the cemetery by the remnants of II./GR 146, comprising no more than two companies. Not only was the attack repulsed, but A Company counter-attacked and came to close combat with fixed bayonets. This turned out not to be the main problem for, at 1800hrs, eight panzers from 8.Kompanie, II./Panzer-Regiment 26 supported by 6.Kompanie, Panzergrenadier-Regiment 9 moved down the Arielli–Orsogna road ignoring the NZ 23rd Battalion and hitting the positions held by C Company, NZ 28th Battalion. Unable to deal effectively with the German armour, C Company had no other choice than to withdraw, enabling the *Panzergrenadiere* to regain the positions they had lost in the afternoon. The panzers almost reached the cemetery before being halted by a 'stonk', a massive concentration of artillery fire.

At 2245hrs, the Germans made another attempt, this time with 6.Kompanie, Panzer-Regiment 26, which moved from the road just north of Orsogna against A Company. The latter, which had been unable to deal with the panzers, withdrew on Wirepa's order to the Pascuccio Ridge. Operation *Torso* had clearly failed, and at 0020hrs on 8 December the entire NZ 28th Battalion withdrew, followed by the NZ 24th Battalion. The NZ 2nd Division's commander, General Freyberg, sanctioned the withdrawal at 0230hrs just as German reinforcements (in the shape of III./FJR 4) deployed at Orsogna. The second New Zealander attack on Orsogna cost some 30 killed, 90 wounded and 30–40 missing, the positions seized by the NZ 23rd Battalion being the only achievement. The Germans lost 14 killed, 40 wounded and some 50 missing.

Although *Torso* was a severe blow to Freyberg, he was still determined to seize Orsogna and accomplish the task he had been given. This led to another plan, Operation *Florence*, a combined infantry–tank attack intended to outflank the town.

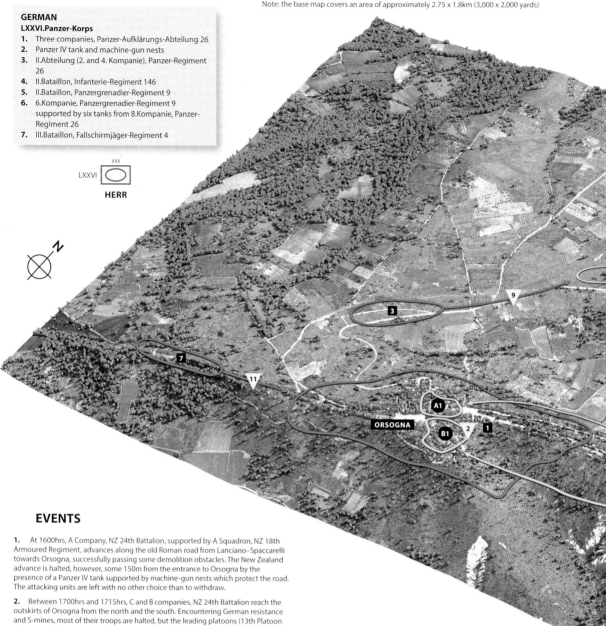

GERMAN
LXXVI.Panzer-Korps
1. Three companies, Panzer-Aufklärungs-Abteilung 26
2. Panzer IV tank and machine-gun nests
3. II.Abteilung (2. and 4. Kompanie), Panzer-Regiment 26
4. II.Bataillon, Infanterie-Regiment 146
5. II.Bataillon, Panzergrenadier-Regiment 9
6. 6.Kompanie, Panzergrenadier-Regiment 9 supported by six tanks from 8.Kompanie, Panzer-Regiment 26
7. III.Bataillon, Fallschirmjäger-Regiment 4

LXXVI
xxx
HERR

ORSOGNA

EVENTS

1. At 1600hrs, A Company, NZ 24th Battalion, supported by A Squadron, NZ 18th Armoured Regiment, advances along the old Roman road from Lanciano–Spaccarelli towards Orsogna, successfully passing some demolition obstacles. The New Zealand advance is halted, however, some 150m from the entrance to Orsogna by the presence of a Panzer IV tank supported by machine-gun nests which protect the road. The attacking units are left with no other choice than to withdraw.

2. Between 1700hrs and 1715hrs, C and B companies, NZ 24th Battalion reach the outskirts of Orsogna from the north and the south. Encountering German resistance and S-mines, most of their troops are halted, but the leading platoons (13th Platoon of C Company, and 10th and 11th platoons of B Company) manage to reach the centre of the town moving along a gully. They soon face a swift reaction from 6.Kompanie, Panzer-Aufklärungs-Abteilung 26 supported by tanks from II.Abteilung, Panzer-Regiment 26, which inflict heavy losses. 10th Platoon is forced to withdraw and seek shelter in a cave; the others withdraw at night.

3. At midnight, in view of the tactical situation and the arrival at Orsogna of III.Bataillon, 4.Fallschirmjäger-Regiment, the three companies of NZ 24th Battalion start their withdrawal, which will be sanctioned at 0230hrs on 8 December by General Freyberg's order.

4. At 1700hrs, the NZ 28th Battalion, led by its D Company, emerges from the Pascuccio Ridge area and attacks 7.Kompanie of Panzergrenadier-Regiment 9, wiping it out. The 28th reaches the Orsogna–Arielli road, where D Company deploys in the cemetery.

5. C Company, NZ 28th Battalion reaches the Orsogna–Arielli road without issue, where it entrenches between there and the railroad.

6. A Company, NZ 28th Battalion, after attacking II.Bataillon, Panzergrenadier-Regiment 9's positions from the rear, advances along the Orsogna–Arielli road to the south, deploying to face a German counter-attack and waiting for the arrival of the NZ 18th Armoured Regiment's tanks.

7. The German counter-attack, led by the remnants of II.Bataillon, Infanterie-Regiment 146 (about two companies strong), materializes soon against the positions held by D Company in the cemetery. D Company repels the counter-attack, and immediately afterwards the Germans are attacked by A Company who are ordered to 'fix bayonets'.

8. At 1800hrs, eight panzers from 8.Kompanie, Panzer-Regiment 26, supported by 6.Kompanie, Panzergrenadier-Regiment 9, after pushing through the positions held by the NZ 23rd Battalion to the north, attack the positions held by C Company, NZ 28th Battalion, compelling it to withdraw and enabling II.Bataillon, Panzergrenadier-Regiment 9 to regain its lost positions. The German advance is then halted by concentrated artillery fire (a 'stonk').

9. At 2245hrs, 6.Kompanie, of Panzer-Regiment 26, advances north along the Orsogna–Arielli road attacking the positions held by C Company, NZ 28th Battalion. The challenging terrain, and mortar and artillery fire halt its advance.

10. Following the withdrawal of C Company and facing German counter-attacks, D Company, followed by A Company, also withdraws at 0020hrs on 8 December.

11. At midnight, the leading company of III.Bataillon, Fallschirmjäger-Regiment 4 reaches Orsogna, securing and consolidating the German positions.

Note: the base map covers an area of approximately 2.75 x 1.8km (3,000 x 2,000 yards)

OPERATION *TORSO*: THE ATTACK ON ORSOGNA, 7–8 DECEMBER 1943

Following the failed attempt to seize Orsogna by the NZ 25th Battalion on 2–3 December, General Freyberg planned a two-pronged attack intending to take the town from the north and the east. The frontal attack, along the old Roman road, was carried out by the NZ 24th Battalion supported by tanks of the NZ 18th Armoured Regiment. To the north, moving across the Pascuccio Ridge, the NZ 28th and 23rd battalions were to secure the road leading to Orsogna, paving the way for the tank attack. The resistance offered by Panzer-Aufklärungs-Bataillon 26 at Orsogna counter-balanced the success of the NZ 28th and 23rd battalions against elements of both 65.Infanterie-Division and 26.Panzer-Division. Even though the German counter-attacks failed, the arrival at Orsogna of III./Fallschirmjäger-Regiment 4 by the end of 7 December brought to an end Operation *Torso*.

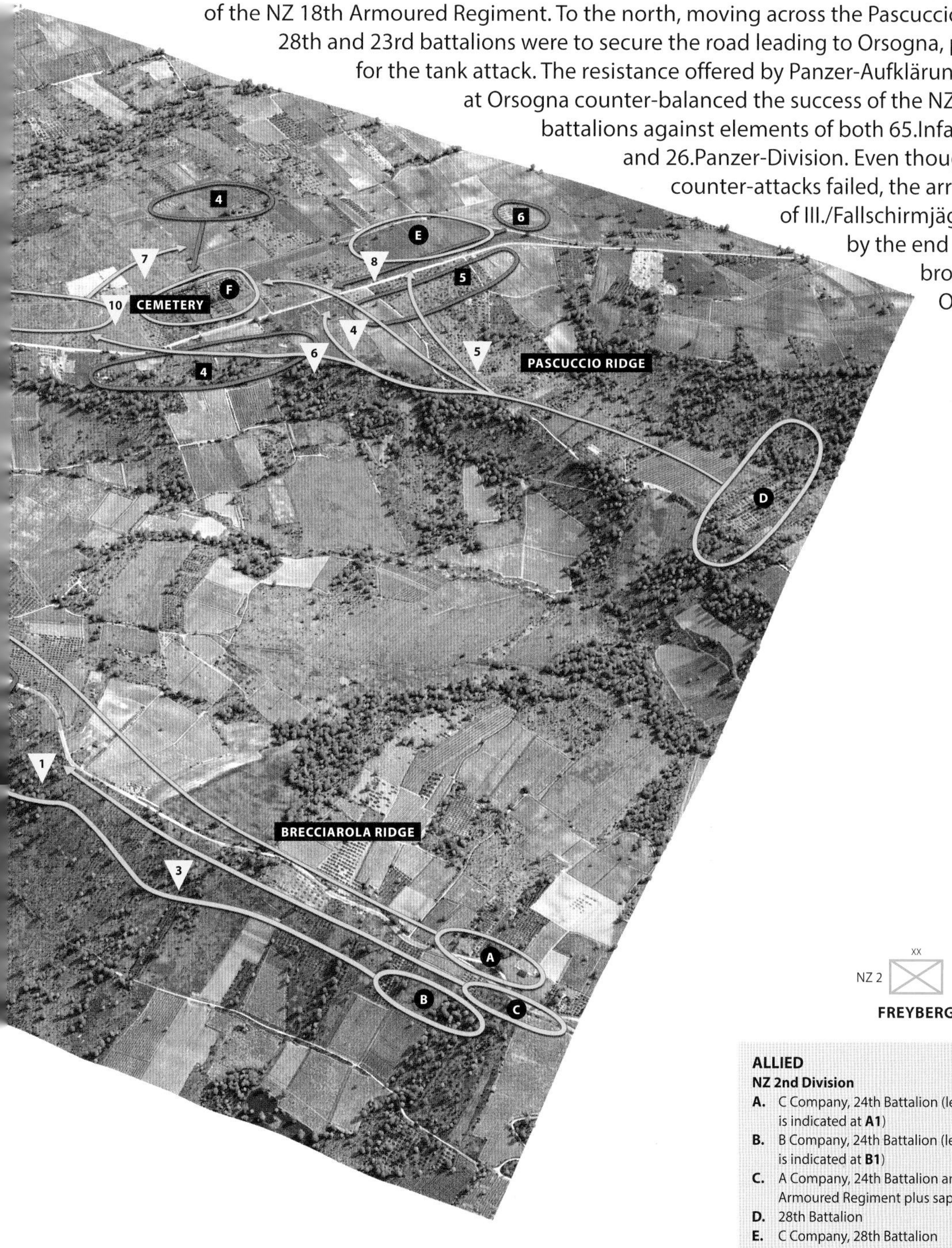

CEMETERY

PASCUCCIO RIDGE

BRECCIAROLA RIDGE

NZ 2

FREYBERG

ALLIED
NZ 2nd Division
A. C Company, 24th Battalion (lead platoon position is indicated at **A1**)
B. B Company, 24th Battalion (lead platoon position is indicated at **B1**)
C. A Company, 24th Battalion and A Squadron, 18th Armoured Regiment plus sappers
D. 28th Battalion
E. C Company, 28th Battalion
F. D Company, 28th Battalion
G. A Company, 28th Battalion

OUTFLANKING ORSOGNA: OPERATION *FLORENCE*

The NZ 23rd Battalion area on Sfasciata Ridge was the only gain by NZ 2nd Division in Operation *Torso* and, having ruled out another direct attack on the town, it was used for the next plan. This time, Orsogna would be outflanked, with the NZ 5th Brigade moving from the Sfasciata Ridge to seize the Orsogna–Arielli road and attack the town from the north. This required improving the track from Spaccarelli (renamed 'Duncan's Road') which, after works carried out on 8–9 December, enabled 28 Sherman tanks from the NZ 18th Armoured Regiment to deploy for the attack. The plan (named Operation *Florence*) required the NZ 21st Battalion to deploy on the right flank along the road while the NZ 23rd Battalion deployed on the left in the cemetery area. The NZ 25th Battalion was to deploy on the Pascuccio Ridge defending the left flank, and enabling the NZ 26th Battalion to attack Orsogna with the support of NZ 18th Armoured Regiment. If successful, the attack was to be followed by the advance of the NZ 28th (Maori) Battalion, supported by the NZ 20th Armoured Regiment.

The plan was in fact part of a major operation intended to break through the German defences as the Canadians attacked across the Moro River. This included a reorganization of command; from 15 December, the NZ 2nd Division was part of BR XIII Corps along with the BR 5th Division, whose 17th Brigade deployed two days later. Planned to begin on 10 December, Operation *Florence* was postponed because of poor weather. It was based on the assumption that, in spite of the failure of Operation *Torso*, it would meet worn-down German defences that would be easy to overcome. It did not take into account that the New Zealander units had also suffered losses, and that the Germans were determined to defend Orsogna. The 65.Infanterie-Division, which had almost been destroyed, was withdrawn from the front to rest and refit on 3 December, leaving the Orsogna area to 26.Panzer-Division. Since the latter, from 5 December, had to take over most of the area formerly held by 90.Panzergrenadier-Division, on 6–7 December 65.Infanterie-Division, now under command of General Hellmuth Pfeifer, was brought back to the front line in the Orsogna area, the town itself being now defended by the men of III./FJR 4.

Operation *Florence* started at 0100hrs on 15 December with the customary hail of artillery fire, the NZ 23rd Battalion (with B Company on the right, D in the centre, A on the left and C in reserve) suffering from friendly fire which wounded the B Company commander. Still, facing little enemy opposition and the withdrawal of two companies of II./PGR 9, by 0200hrs, the battalion deployed along the road to Arielli north of the cemetery. Only A Company, moving towards the cemetery to link up with the NZ 25th Battalion, encountered significant German resistance and artillery fire,

An SdKfz 8 tractor, recovering a damaged Panzer IV Ausf. G, makes its way along a mountain road in central Italy in November 1943. (Narodowe Archiwum Cyfrowe)

which caused heavy losses, reducing the battalion's combat strength to 23 per cent of its establishment. The battalion commander, Lieutenant-Colonel R.E. Romans, was seriously wounded and died two days later. To the Germans the situation was so critical that II./GR 146 was brought forward at once.

Even though it faced German resistance from II./PGR 67 blocking its advance, the NZ 21st Battalion (with D Company on the right, A in the centre, B on the left and C in reserve) managed to reach the road at 0245–0300hrs, still under enemy fire. The situation took a turn for the worse over the next few hours. At 0500hrs, three Panzer IVs

Two German soldiers cautiously move into a wooded gully. The difficult terrain also hindered communications amongst the defenders, all too often isolating single strongpoints. (Narodowe Archiwum Cyfrowe)

from 8.Kompanie, Panzer-Regiment 26 attacked from Arielli the positions held by B Company, NZ 21st Battalion, which withdrew followed by A Company. The panzers advanced along the road to the positions held by B Company, NZ 23rd Battalion, but were stopped thanks to the heroic deeds of Private Bob Clay who, using a PIAT, hit the leading panzer and forced its abandonment. The German armour withdrew, but the New Zealanders were hit by friendly artillery fire. Clay would be killed in action that same day.

At 0515hrs, the Shermans of NZ 18th Armoured Regiment approached the road; many of them halted on the unsuitable track. Only one tank, led by Major Horton, from C Squadron reached the road, deploying on the right flank, A Squadron tanks deployed on the left flank between Sfasciata Ridge and the positions held by the NZ 23rd Battalion. Without infantry support, A Squadron's commander, Captain Burns, advanced towards Orsogna reaching the cemetery, before being ordered to turn back to join Horton in defence of the NZ 21st Battalion. At 0900hrs, two Panzer IVs supported by a Panzergrenadier platoon attacked again from Arielli, compelling D Company, NZ 21st Battalion to withdraw. One of the panzers was destroyed at dawn by a Sherman, forcing the other to pull back at 0930hrs.

As B Squadron, NZ 18th Armoured Regiment reached the road and joined up with A Squadron, bringing the total number of Shermans to 14 (out of 28), Brigadier Kippenberger, NZ 5th Brigade's commander, ordered a reconnaissance towards Orsogna. At 1300hrs, once again without infantry support, the tanks moved out, but one Sherman hit a mine some 100m south of the cemetery, blocking the road and stopping the entire action. The arrival at 1400hrs in the cemetery area of A and C squadrons, NZ 20th Armoured Regiment (bringing the number of Shermans available to 28) made another attempt possible. The NZ 28th Battalion was supposed to join the tanks but was delayed (it eventually reached the area at 2100hrs), so the tanks moved ahead at 1600hrs without infantry. Almost immediately, the leading Sherman was hit by an 88mm gun hidden west of Orsogna. Two other tanks were also hit, but C Squadron kept advancing across the positions held by II./GR 146, almost reaching Orsogna's rear gateways. Only 14.Panzerjäger-Kompanie of III./FJR 4 managed to halt them, along with three Panzer IVs, two of which were destroyed.

German *Pioniere* laying down a barbed-wire obstacle. These obstacles could be formidable, especially when covered by machine-gun positions. (Narodowe Archiwum Cyfrowe)

Left with eight tanks in running order and no infantry, C Squadron withdrew to the cemetery, being joined there at 1730hrs by A Squadron. At the end of the day, the NZ 18th Armoured Regiment was left with 13 tanks, and the 20th with 23. Facing a difficult situation, General Lüttwitz sent reinforcements, in particular III./FJR 6 led by Major Pelz. This, supported by the tanks of 7.Kompanie, Panzer-Regiment 26 (four Panzer IVs, five Panzer III Flammenwerfer and three Italian self-propelled guns) attacked from Arielli the NZ 21st Battalion's positions. The prompt reaction of A and B squadrons, NZ 18th Armoured Regiment saw two Panzer IVs and one Panzer III hit, the latter's flames revealing its position which led to it being destroyed. As the Fallschirmjäger attacked A Company and D Company, NZ 23rd Battalion's positions, heavy mortar and artillery fire rained down on them. Eventually, the Germans called the attack off at 0630hrs, leaving behind six of their panzers.

The arrival of the NZ 28th Battalion, which relieved the NZ 23rd, prompted another attack towards Orsogna planned by the Maori's commander Colonel Fairbrother, acting on Kippenberger's request. At 0700hrs on the 16th, the attack started with C Squadron, NZ 20th Regiment (comprising seven Shermans, with the regiment under the command of Colonel McKergow) advancing to the left of the road along with D Company, NZ 28th Battalion; and with A Squadron, NZ 20th Regiment (ten Shermans) to the right along with A Company, NZ 28th Battalion. One tank was hit about 1km south of the cemetery. As two others were also hit, the Maoris came under machine-gun fire. At 1155hrs, the tanks and infantry withdrew. Having lost four tanks, A Squadron's remaining armour approached Orsogna's northern end, but since the tanks could not move off-road because of the terrain, the attack was called off at 1130hrs. Nine Shermans in total had been destroyed.

STALEMATE

Further attempts were made on 17 and 18 December towards Orsogna and Arielli by the tanks of the NZ 18th and 20th Armoured regiments, supported by the NZ 21st and 26th battalions. The first was driven off by the Germans, the second found the area already secured by elements of the BR 5th Division. The only gain of Operation *Florence* was the creation of an advanced front line, which could allow the German defences to be pierced while ignoring Orsogna.

On Montgomery's orders, the NZ 2nd and BR 5th divisions were to attack between Orsogna and Arielli in the Fontegrande Ridge area. Operation *Ulysses*, which saw the NZ 5th Brigade moving from the Orsogna–Arielli road with the NZ 21st Battalion to the right and the NZ 28th to the left, plus the NZ 26th Battalion, supported by B Squadron, 20th Armoured Regiment started at 0400hrs on 24 December. The NZ 21st Battalion's advance was halted at the

German defensive line on the Fontegrande Ridge, while the NZ 26th Battalion reached the Fontanagrande Creek at 0415hrs before halting. Paving the way for the Shermans of NZ 20th Armoured Regiment, the NZ 28th Battalion faced unfavourable terrain which halted both its advance and that of the tanks. The latter eventually withdrew at 2200hrs, putting an end to Operation *Ulysses*, which only brought the New Zealanders' advanced front line closer to the main German defensive line. The operation cost the Allies 119 losses, the Germans 75.

This was the last action in the Orsogna area, the NZ 2nd Division being later transferred to the Cassino front. The town would not be seized until the final breakthrough of the Gustav Line in May 1944.

THE ADVANCE FROM THE MORO RIVER

Trooper E. Mossman (left) and Trooper E.B. Smith, who came under German mortar fire during the fighting in the Orsogna area, examine their damaged helmets, both of which received shrapnel hits. (© Imperial War Museum, NA 9993)

On 4 December, General Vokes, CDN 1st Infantry Division's commander, accelerated his plans following news of the Indian advance to Frisia and of the New Zealanders' failed attempt at Orsogna. To speed things up, Vokes ordered a reconnaissance to Villa Rogatti, which reported the Moro River to be fordable, and to the road east of San Leonardo, where the river was reported more difficult to cross. As he ordered a crossing of the Moro south of San Leonardo, Vokes planned the battle for Ortona. Once a bridgehead was secured, exploitation would be directed either to the west, towards Tollo, or to the east, towards Ortona. Much would depend on developments on the battlefield.

ALLIED ORDER OF BATTLE, ORTONA

CDN 1st Infantry Division (Major-General Christopher Vokes)
1st Infantry Brigade (Brigadier Henry D. Graham, from 16 December Brigadier Daniel C. Spry)
    The Royal Canadian Regiment (RCR)
    The Hastings and Prince Edward Regiment (HPER)
    48th Highlanders of Canada (48th HOC)
2nd Infantry Brigade (Brigadier Bertram M. Hoffmeister)
    Princess Patricia's Canadian Light Infantry (PPCLI)
    The Seaforth Highlanders of Canada (SHC)
    The Loyal Edmonton Regiment (LER)
3rd Infantry Brigade (Brigadier Thomas G. Gibson)
    Royal 22e Régiment (R22e)
    The Carleton and York Regiment (CYR)
    The West Nova Scotia Regiment (WNSR)

1st Canadian Armoured Brigade (Brigadier Robert A. Wyman)
    The Ontario Regiment (11th Armoured Regiment)
    Three Rivers Regiment (12th Armoured Regiment) (TRR)
    The Calgary Regiment (14th Armoured Regiment)
4th Reconnaissance Regiment (Princess Louise Dragoon Guards)
Divisional Artillery
    1st Field Regiment, Royal Canadian Horse Artillery
    2nd Field Regiment, Royal Canadian Artillery
    3rd Field Regiment, Royal Canadian Artillery
    1st Anti-Tank Regiment, Royal Canadian Artillery
    2nd Light Anti-Aircraft Regiment, Royal Canadian Artillery
The Saskatoon Light Infantry (machine-gun battalion)
1st–4th companies, Royal Canadian Engineers

In detail, the CDN 2nd Brigade was ordered to attack to the south of CDN 1st Infantry Division's area, while the CDN 1st Brigade carried out a diversionary move on the right flank. The PPCLI was to cross at Villa Rogatti, the SHC east of San Leonardo and the HPER was to cross near the coast in the San Donato area.[3] To achieve surprise, there would be no artillery barrage, although the artillery would remain on call. At midnight on 6 December, the PPCLI crossed the river taking elements from Panzergrenadier-Regiment 200 by surprise, which enabled the seizure of Villa Rogatti by daylight, even though it remained under German artillery fire. The SHC also easily crossed the Moro, but faced stubborn German resistance as its troops approached San Leonardo. This merely enabled, by 0500hrs, the creation of a small bridgehead while, at 0900hrs, the Germans counter-attacked at Villa Rogatti. The attack was eventually repulsed 2½ hours later thanks to the arrival of the tanks of CDN 4th Armoured Brigade, but since the SHC was unable to extend the bridgehead, the advance stalled. The PPCLI was considered for an attack against the road junction west of San Leonardo, but the plan was cancelled given the lack of suitable roads in its area.

HPER's crossing near the coast faced at first a German reaction before a prompt withdrawal. Nevertheless, the battalion established a bridgehead before attacking at 1400hrs Panzergrenadier-Regiment 361's positions. The German reaction led to a withdrawal order, which was not received by D Company; it continued to advance, eventually being followed by the other companies which, by 2000hrs had reached the road junction just south of San Donato. This success did not change the situation, and the plan was altered. The IND 8th Division was to relieve the PPCLI at Villa Rogatti, which it did

---

3 Abbreviations are used for Canadian units throughout this subchapter. An explanatory list is provided on page 2 of this work, and in the Order of Battle listing in this subchapter.

at midnight on the 7th, while the CDN 1st Brigade would now focus on the seizure of San Leonardo and the CDN 2nd Brigade was to exploit the success.

Apart from the SHC, the attack included the 48th HOC crossing to the south towards La Torre and the RCR, which was to join the HPER, to attack San Leonardo from the north. The objective, the road junction to Ortona, seemed within grasp considering that good weather enabled air support and that the fresh CDN 1st Armoured Brigade had replaced the 4th Armoured Brigade. Not everything went according to plan, however. At 0430hrs on the 8th, the RCR attacked from the coastal bridgehead, only to run head into a German counter-attack. Following the ensuing hard fight, the plan suffered a delay and the RCR's advance was halted at about

2200hrs at a house north-east of San Leonardo. Another German counter-attack was beaten off by the artillery, but the RCR's hold on its position was fragile. Things went better for the 48th HOC, which crossed the Moro with ease and established a bridgehead.

On 9 December, as the Shermans of CDN 1st Armoured Brigade crossed the river, the Germans were still in San Leonardo. The SHC, with tank support, attacked it at 1000hrs, and soon faced a German counter-attack, which did not prevent it from seizing the town and securing it by 1740hrs. The use of 90.Panzergrenadier-Division's reserves to attack the 48th HOC and the HPER in the coastal zone surely helped the taking of San Leonardo. The German attack having ended in failure, the Canadians were able to establish a firm bridgehead on the Moro from San Donato to San Leonardo. This left few alternatives to General Herr, 90.Panzergrenadier Division's units being already understrength before the Canadian attack. The 26.Panzer-Division deployed Panzergrenadier-Regiment 9, its last reserve, and took over part of 90.Panzergrenadier-Division's area. A withdrawal became necessary and, most importantly, the last units were thrown into battle. The first available elements from 1.Fallschirmjäger-Division, its bulk deployed on LXXVI.Panzer-Korps' western flank, were ordered to the Ortona area on 9 December, and on 11–13 December III. and II./FJR 3 along with II./FJR 1 deployed in 90.Panzergrenadier-Division's area of responsibility.

The advance from the Moro was to see the CDN 2nd Brigade move towards the Orsogna–Ortona road, with the SHC moving towards Casa Berardi on the left flank, the LER seizing the main crossroads (known as 'Cider') in the centre and the PPCLI on the right flank. The LER moved off at 0900hrs on the 9th, making a rapid advance and reaching the 'Cider' crossroads, only to be driven back by a counter-attack from Panzergrenadier-Regiment 200. Communication problems saw the PPCLI moving off behind schedule and, by the next day, the SHC, LER and PPCLI were all halted at

Lieutenant I. Macdonald (using binoculars) checks the tactical situation before ordering his men from the 48th HOC to attack in the Casa Berardi area, the cornerstone of the battle on the way to Ortona. (Public domain)

the gully before the road by the German resistance. The HPER advanced most rapidly along the coast, reaching the gully some 2.5km south of Ortona, while the 48th HOC seized La Torre.

The gully was clearly the new German line of resistance, and to deal with it Vokes committed his last reserves – the CDN 3rd Brigade. Still, the WNSR's move across the SHC's positions and the subsequent attack towards Casa Berardi at 1800hrs on the 11th ended in failure, compelling Vokes to order the CDN 3rd Brigade to make another frontal attack. Consequently, the CYR was to attack south of the PPCLI's positions while the WNSR made another attempt on Casa Berardi and one company of the R22e moved from the La Torre area to attack the southern end of the German line.

The German resistance exhausted the Canadian units' attacks in about an hour, and the lack of reserves did not permit an exploitation of the minor successes achieved, as in the case of A Company, SHC towards Casa Berardi. While the units of 1.Fallschirmjäger-Division restored the German defensive line along the gully, on 13 December the R22e was fully committed, leaving no other unit available. In the meantime, even the IND 8th Division was slowed in its advance from Villa Rogatti towards Villa Caldari and Villa Jubatti.

Between 13 and 15 December, the battle focused on Casa Berardi, and Vokes developed a pincer plan with the R22e attacking along the crossroads from the south-west, while the PPCLI was to attack frontally. As the men of the R22e deployed to attack, the Germans counter-attacked; the Canadians managed to advance thanks only to a PIAT destroying a Panzer IV. Having been on the move since 1030hrs, the Canadians faced strong German opposition, but this did not prevent them from seizing Casa Berardi in the late afternoon on the 14th. All other units maintained pressure on the Germans but made no gains; however, as the Canadians were now close to the 'Cider' crossroads, exploitation became possible. As the Germans committed their last unit (III./FJR 6 redeployed from Orsogna), at 0730hrs on 15 December the CYR attacked towards the crossroads, before being halted after some 200m. This marked the end of the attempts against the gully from the east, the focus switching now to Casa Berardi (where the Germans counter-attacked that same afternoon, without success) and the Orsogna–Ortona road.

A minor redeployment took place, with the 48th HOC ordered to move south of Casa Berardi towards the north-east, in the direction of the Villa Grande road. The RCR was to follow it, advancing towards 'Cider' from the same direction, while the HPER was to advance north east of the Riccio River towards San Tommaso and San Nicola. The second phase of the Canadian attack was to have the CDN 2nd Brigade seizing Ortona.

The attack, dubbed 'Morning Glory', started at 0800hrs on 18 December with a heavy artillery barrage. The 48th HOC advanced to the north-west, reaching the

A Jeep ambulance of the Royal Canadian Army Medical Corps brings in two wounded soldiers from the San Leonardo area, on 10 December 1943. Jeeps were more suitable than ambulances in the Moro River area, given the poor roads and the constant German shelling. (Public domain)

road at 1030hrs. Suffering friendly fire, the RCR's advance was halted by the Fallschirmjäger's fierce defence before the 'Cider' crossroads. Attacking again the next day at 1415hrs, the RCR was able to advance as the Fallschirmjäger pulled back. The 'Cider' crossroads was easily seized at 1700hrs on the 19th, opening the way for CDN 2nd Brigade's advance towards Ortona. The LER crossed the bridge on the road and reached the town's outskirts at 1426hrs, followed on its right flank by the SHC. On 20 December, the front line extended from the Villa Grande road to the 'Cider' crossroads, the Orsogna–Ortona road and Ortona.

A German command post protected by wood and covered with a Zeltbahn (shelter-half). The Leutnant is giving references using a map being helped by the Feldwebel on the left. (Narodowe Archiwum Cyfrowe)

As the CDN 2nd Brigade focused on Ortona, the final part of the battle (lasting from 22 December 1943 to 4 January 1944) was fought on the Riccio salient with the aim of isolating Ortona. On 20 December, as the IND 8th Division was halted before Villa Grande, the CDN 1st Brigade redeployed; it launched an attack three days later with the HPER advancing east of the Riccio, and the 48th HOC following and advancing to San Nicola and San Tommaso. The RCR was to make the final advance to the coast, towards Torre Mucchia.

The HPER attacked from the Casa Berardi area at 0930hrs on the 23rd, reaching its objective the next day. As planned, the 48th HOC followed, seizing its objective in the morning of the 24th, even though the two battalions were unable to make contact because of III./FJR 3's defence. This required a change of plan, but as the two battalions tried to establish a link, at 1000hrs on 26 December they were attacked by III./FJR 1. After repulsing the German attack, the 48th HOC advanced to the eastern bank of the Riccio, eventually seizing San Tommaso and San Nicola. With the IND 8th Division seizing Villa Grande on 28 December, the Germans had no other alternative than to withdraw to Torre Mucchia, which enabled the R22e to advance towards Tollo and the CYR towards Torre Mucchia.

A Sherman tank of the Three Rivers Regiment (12th Armoured Regiment, CDN 1st Armoured Brigade), stuck in the mud at the Arielli River in January 1944. (© Imperial War Museum, NA 11136)

On 29 December, German resistance once again halted the Canadian advance, a signal that there would be no collapse of the enemy defences. On 30 December, the R22e seized their objective of the crossroads east of the Riccio, while the CYR made repeated attempts against Torre Mucchia, defended by I./FJR 1. It would be eventually seized on 4 January 1944, marking the end of BR Eighth Army's offensive on the Adriatic. It cost the CDN 1st Infantry Division a total of 2,339 men.

The Battle for Ortona, 5 December 1943–19 January 1944

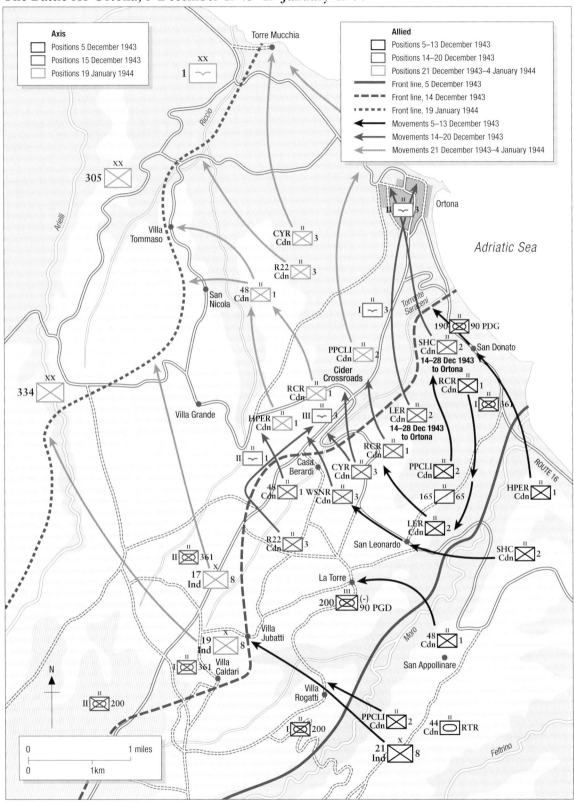

ORTONA: THE FIRST PHASE

General Vokes' decision to exploit towards Ortona rather than Tollo is questionable, to say the least. A town of fewer than 10,000 inhabitants built on a promontory, it controlled the coastal road (Route 16), but this could have been bypassed. Only its swift seizure could pave the way for an advance along the coast.

Apart from the underdeveloped outskirts, Ortona's centre was characterized by narrow streets and roads, all interlocked one with another. This offered its Axis defenders many advantages, which Hauptmann Gotthart Liebscher, II./FJR 3's commander, readily exploited. Supported by elements from Fallschirm-Pioniere-Bataillon 1 and Fallschirm-Panzerjäger-Abteilung 1, Liebscher planned a defence of the town's outskirts at the main buildings. The old town, lying at its centre, was carefully exploited to prepare a trap. Seven out of the ten roads inside the old town were blocked by piles of rubble, usually 3–5m high, created by destroying buildings or parts of them. This was intended to funnel the attackers into a series of 'killing zones', comprising the main squares inside the old town and in particular the market square close to the cathedral.

Lacking manpower and resources, the reported strength of II./FJR 3 varies from 180 to 200, to which non-combat elements should be added along with elements from Pioniere and Panzerjäger units; Liebscher heavily relied on the work of the former. Many houses were booby trapped, from the doors to small elements in the interiors (like toilet flushes), others were mined to be blown up when full of enemy troops. The few PAK guns available were deployed to cover the squares and, most importantly, the Fallschirmjäger relied on a series of underground tunnels to move undetected at will. Both II./FJR 3 and Hauptmann Karl Vosshage's II./FJR 4 (with a reported strength of 150) took shelter in the railway tunnel under construction at the northern end of the town. Moving by night, or using the tunnels, they shifted small groups of men from one part of the town to another by stealth, avoiding enemy fire. It is estimated that no more than 100 Fallschirmjäger at a time fought in Ortona.

For the taking of Ortona, the CDN 2nd Brigade, commanded by Brigadier Bertram Hoffmeister, employed the LER commanded by Lieutenant-Colonel Jim C. Jefferson, and the SHC commanded by Major (Lieutenant-Colonel from 22 December) Syd Thomson; both units had an average strength of over 600. They were supported by the Sherman tanks of the 12th TRR, 1st Armoured Brigade, usually operating in one- or two-tank troops. Other support troops included the 4th Field Company of the Royal Canadian Engineers, and the 90th Anti-Tank Battery of the Royal Canadian Artillery, whose 17-pdr guns proved extremely effective against Ortona's houses. Divisional artillery

An aerial reconnaissance photograph of Ortona taken before the battle. The battle for Ortona's old town began at noon on 22 December, as D Company, LER, supported by the Shermans of 2nd Troop, C Squadron, TRR, began its advance along Corso Vittorio Emanuele II (named after one of Italy's kings) with the aim of reaching the central Piazza Municipale. The length from the southern entrance of Corso Vittorio Emanuele II to Piazza Municipale is about 250m. (Public domain)

Canadian troops from D Company, SHC approaching the entrance to Via Rapino from Piazza della Vittoria. This photo was likely taken on 22 December 1943. (NARA via Digital History Archive)

also provided fire support, in particular against the northern end of the town. Since Canadian intelligence estimated that the Germans would not defend Ortona, basically no plan was devised other than having the LER moving across town via Route 16/Corso Vittorio Emanuele inside the town itself, which was the only two-way paved road available.

The battle of Ortona began at 1200hrs on 20 December, as the CDN 3rd Field Artillery Regiment started a creeping barrage behind which two tank troops from C Squadron, TRR advanced along with B and D companies, LER, and C and D companies, SHC. When one Sherman was destroyed by an explosive device on the road, the others discovered that this was deliberately intended to drive them off-road into a minefield – where three other tanks had their tracks destroyed. Nevertheless, the remaining Sherman and the LER companies pressed on, approaching the German trenches just south of the town. After a brief exchange of fire, the Germans withdrew. At 1426hrs, the LER reached its objective, a guesthouse at the southern end of Ortona soon named 'Johnson's House'.

To their right the SHC faced strong German resistance, with machine-gun fire coming from a crest to the south of the church of Santa Maria. The Canadian attack was followed by a counter-attack, and yet another attack. By the end of the day, as the Canadians consolidated their positions, the SHC was still 300m away from the church, with German machine-gun nests relentlessly firing on the attackers.

At 0700hrs on 21 December, the blast of a huge explosion surprised everybody. The San Tommaso cathedral had been blown up by the Germans, who later claimed it was an accident. This did not halt the Canadians, whose approach to the town continued. D and B companies, LER, each supported by a tank troop, advanced up the central Corso Michele Bianchi, but faced different situations. On the right flank, B Company advanced easily, while on the left D Company was halted at Johnson's House by German fire. After suffering severe losses, the remaining men of D Company successfully attacked the house, which was seized just before the two companies linked up. This enabled B Company to continue to advance along Corso Michele Bianchi.

On the right flank the SHC's C Company attacked the Santa Maria church again, struggling to approach because of German mortar and sniper fire. Skilled approach tactics reduced the Canadian losses to just seven casualties, even though it took most of the day to reach and clear the church, paving the way for an advance along Via Constantinopoli. For this task, Hoffmeister ordered the entire SHC battalion be committed, with one company attached to the LER. The SHC's C Company, supported by the Shermans of C Squadron,

TRR, advanced from the church and along Via Constantinopoli, making good use of its armoured support. At the end of the day, the leading SHC troops reached the area just south of Piazza della Vittoria.

D and B companies, LER, supported by D Company, SHC advancing on their left flank and by the tanks of the TRR (one troop, C Squadron), advanced along Corso Michele Bianchi, the infantry carefully clearing all the houses to protect the Sherman. It took the entire day to advance some 350m, with many casualties being caused by booby traps; the infantry–tank co-operation enabled them to deal swiftly with any German machine-gun nests. As the Canadians approached the old town, Hoffmeister had a clear view of the kind of battle that would be fought. After moving his headquarters to Ortona's outskirts, Hoffmeister realized he could not control the battle and decided to establish a routine of daily visits to the front line. Even though there was little he could actually do, these visits enabled him to maintain a modicum of control while boosting the morale of his men.

At the end of the day, the LER reached Piazza della Vittoria, capturing two anti-tank guns and one mortar and taking several prisoners. The Canadians took some time to rest and refit, knowing that hard fighting still lay ahead of them.

After reaching Piazza della Vittoria, Sergeant Jimmy Marchand's Sherman fired its main gun. As he poked his head and shoulders out of the turret to observe, a German sniper fired, wounding him. He was subsequently treated by the medics seen here, who took him to safety. (NARA via Digital History Archive)

Note: the base map covers an area of approximately 1 x 1.57km (1,094 x 1,718 yards)

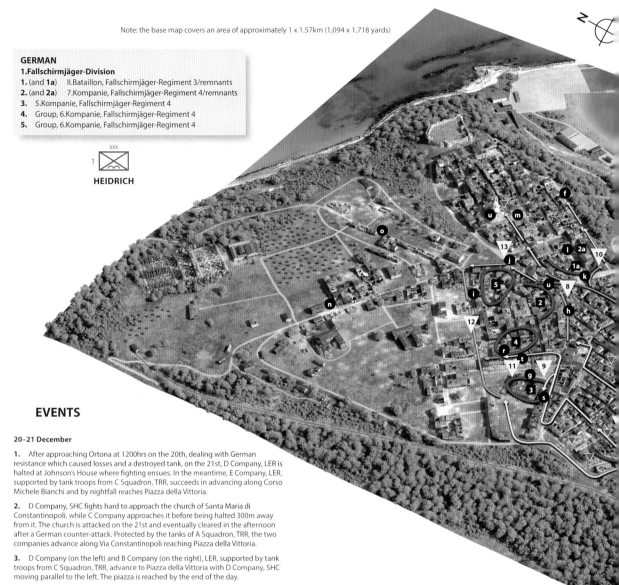

GERMAN

1.Fallschirmjäger-Division

1. (and **1a**) II.Bataillon, Fallschirmjäger-Regiment 3/remnants
2. (and **2a**) 7.Kompanie, Fallschirmjäger-Regiment 4/remnants
3. 5.Kompanie, Fallschirmjäger-Regiment 4
4. Group, 6.Kompanie, Fallschirmjäger-Regiment 4
5. Group, 6.Kompanie, Fallschirmjäger-Regiment 4

HEIDRICH

EVENTS

20–21 December

1. After approaching Ortona at 1200hrs on the 20th, dealing with German resistance which caused losses and a destroyed tank, on the 21st, D Company, LER is halted at Johnson's House where fighting ensues. In the meantime, E Company, LER, supported by tank troops from C Squadron, TRR, succeeds in advancing along Corso Michele Bianchi and by nightfall reaches Piazza della Vittoria.

2. D Company, SHC fights hard to approach the church of Santa Maria di Constantinopoli, while C Company approaches it before being halted 300m away from it. The church is attacked on the 21st and eventually cleared in the afternoon after a German counter-attack. Protected by the tanks of A Squadron, TRR, the two companies advance along Via Constantinopoli reaching Piazza della Vittoria.

3. D Company (on the left) and B Company (on the right), LER, supported by tank troops from C Squadron, TRR, advance to Piazza della Vittoria with D Company, SHC moving parallel to the left. The piazza is reached by the end of the day.

22 December

4. The LER (A Company left, D Company right, B Company along Corso Garibaldi, supported by one tank troop from C Squadron, TRR) carry out 'stone penetration', their thrust aiming at advancing along Corso Vittorio Emanuele and Corso Garibaldi at the same time. When the rubble pile is reached, the German resistance compels A and D companies to seek refuge in the houses.

5. The entire SHC Regiment reaches Piazza della Vittoria, where its tactical HQ is established.

6. D Company, SHC begins advancing along Via Rapino in the late evening.

23–25 December

7. Protecting the LER left flank, B Company, SHC is deployed west of Corso Vittorio Emanuele while A Company advances on the fourth parallel road from the corso and D Company along the sixth road.

8. The LER starts carrying out mouseholing, clearing the buildings and eventually reaching Piazza Municipale with both A and D companies. At the same time, B Company moves to the left reaching the entrance to Corso Umberto I. The Piazza Municipale is cleared late at night on 23 December.

9. B Company, SHC follows A Company, taking over while A Company continues its advance. On the 23rd, A Company reaches the edge of Piazza San Francesco ('Dead Horse Square'), taking the school where one section is killed when the building blows up. On the morning of 24 December, a German counter-attack follows, leading to hard fighting inside the cathedral of Santa Maria after the destruction of its bell tower from where a German machine-gun has been firing. At the end of the day, D Company, SHC is on the west side of the piazza, A Company holds its southern portion and B Company its south-east corner. C Squadron, TRR, is now assigned to the SHC, which receives A Squadron in replacement.

26–27 December

10. D Company, LER reaches Piazza Plebiscito facing German anti-tank defences, and a hard fight ensues until the afternoon, when the piazza is seized and the PAK 38 gun eliminated. A Company, LER advances along the northern section of Corso Vittorio Emanuele, eventually reaching the cathedral of San Tommaso, finding it heavily defended by the Germans. The company manages to gain control of the south-west entrance to Piazza San Tommaso. B Company, LER advances along Corso Umberto I, whose buildings are pounded by tank and artillery fire, on 26 December. On the 27th, a building close to the cathedral is blown up, killing 19 men of a platoon of A Company; four other men are injured, and one is found alive on the 30th. D Company advances from Piazza Plebiscito to link up with the SHC on 27 December, reaching the southern end of Via Tripoli by the end of the day. In the meantime, A and B companies secure Piazza San Tommaso.

11. On the 26th, elements from 5. and 6.Kompanie, Fallschirmjäger-Regiment 4 counter-attack at 'Dead Horse Square', infiltrating the positions of B Company, SHC on the west side of the square, of C Company in the centre, of A Company to the east and of D Company to the south. The Germans infiltrate into the cathedral of Santa Maria delle Grazie and into the hospital, cutting off C Company and capturing two sections before withdrawing at noon. The Canadian soldiers are released.

12. On the 26th, B Company, SHC advances along Via Monte Maiella followed by C Company, while A Company advances along Via Cavour (D Company mops up the 'Dead Horse Square' area). The advance of B and C companies is halted by 1700hrs some 100m before Piazza Plebiscito, while A Company reaches Piazza Municipale.

13. On 27 December, D Company, SHC relieves B Company carrying out the advance to Piazza Plebiscito along with C Company. Tanks cannot enter the piazza. German resistance halts the advance, until in the evening D and C companies link up with the LER at the southern end of Via Tripoli. At 2230hrs that same day, the Germans withdraw from Ortona.

78

THE BATTLE FOR ORTONA, 20–28 DECEMBER 1943

On 20 December 1943, the men of the LER and of the SHC attacked the southern outskirts of Ortona, which was defended by II./FJR 3, later to be joined by II./FJR 4. Supported by the tanks of the TRR, the Canadians made their way into Ortona fighting (often house to house) through an almost completely destroyed town, with roads blocked by piles of rubble. The battle, which would become known as the 'Italian Stalingrad', saw the Canadians taking control of Ortona after a week, but with high casualties.

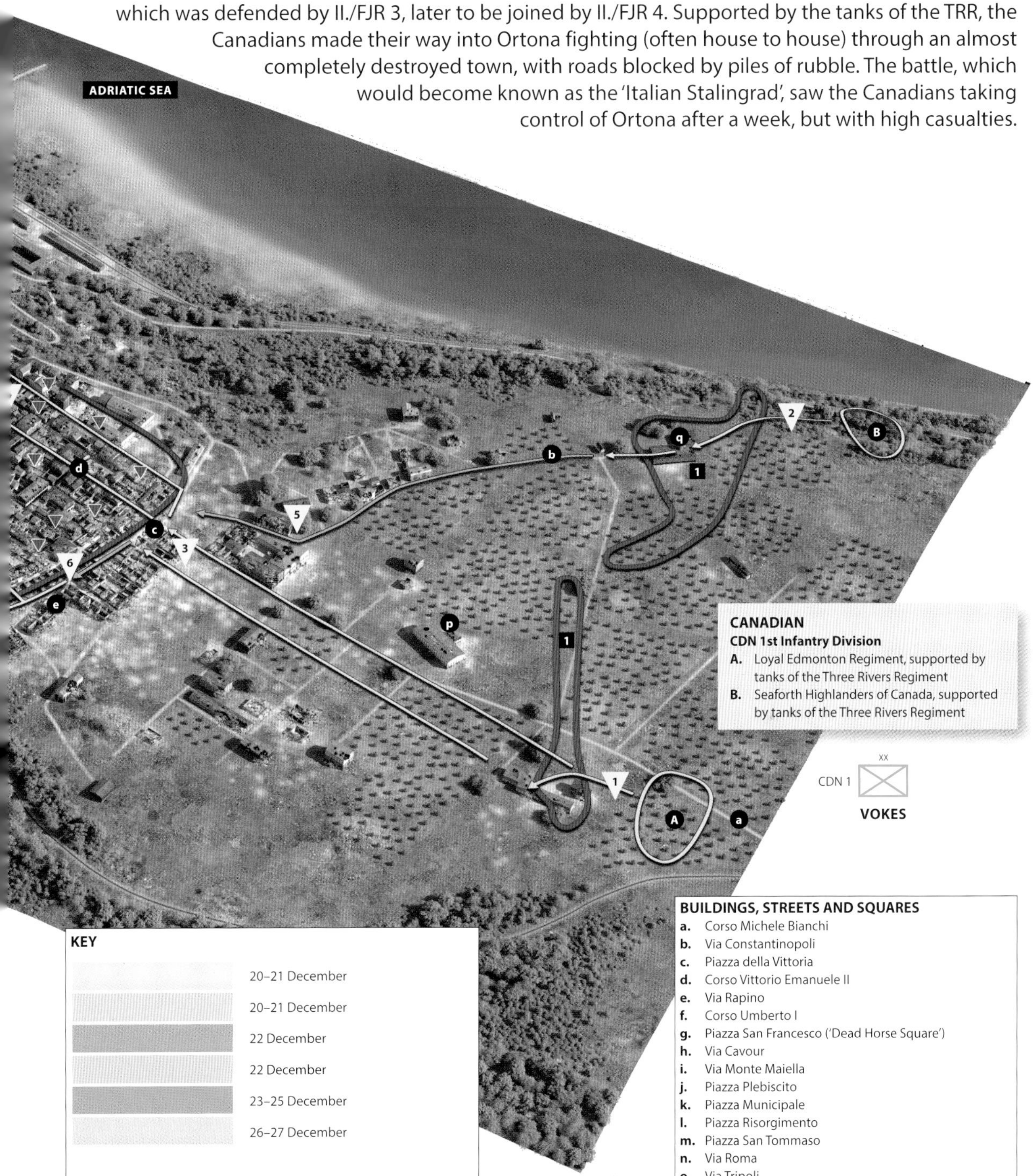

ADRIATIC SEA

CANADIAN

CDN 1st Infantry Division

A. Loyal Edmonton Regiment, supported by tanks of the Three Rivers Regiment

B. Seaforth Highlanders of Canada, supported by tanks of the Three Rivers Regiment

CDN 1   VOKES

KEY

	20–21 December
	20–21 December
	22 December
	22 December
	23–25 December
	26–27 December
	German (movements shown relate to the 25 December counter-attack)
	Rubble obstacle

BUILDINGS, STREETS AND SQUARES

a. Corso Michele Bianchi
b. Via Constantinopoli
c. Piazza della Vittoria
d. Corso Vittorio Emanuele II
e. Via Rapino
f. Corso Umberto I
g. Piazza San Francesco ('Dead Horse Square')
h. Via Cavour
i. Via Monte Maiella
j. Piazza Plebiscito
k. Piazza Municipale
l. Piazza Risorgimento
m. Piazza San Tommaso
n. Via Roma
o. Via Tripoli
p. Johnson's House ('pensione')
q. Church of Santa Maria di Constantinopoli
r. Hospital
s. Cathedral of Santa Maria
t. School
u. Cathedral of San Tommaso

Canadian troops during the bitter fighting in Ortona's outskirts, which saw the Loyal Edmonton Regiment advancing along the main Corso Michele Bianchi and the Seaforth Highlanders of Canada advancing from the Santa Maria church along the Via Constantinopoli. (NARA via Digital History Archive)

FIGHTING INTO ORTONA

On 22 December, the Canadians started their penetration into the old town, from the town gates at Piazza della Vittoria. Since the central Corso Vittorio Emanuele II was found to be clear of rubble, at least until near to Piazza Municipale, it became the obvious route for the penetration of the town. This was carried out by the LER, which Lieutenant-Colonel Jefferson deployed with A Company on the left side and D Company to the right, while B Company would move along the nearest main street on the right flank, Corso Garibaldi. C Company was split, its men being used to reinforce the others along with engineers and anti-tank guns, and a TRR tank troop. The SHC's D Company, attached, would move along the lateral Via Rapino to Ortona's western outskirts.

The Shermans were extremely useful in clearing Piazza della Vittoria, firing on German machine-gun and sniper positions while infantry cleared the area house by house. Once the piazza was cleared, the tactics changed:

Men from C Company, SHC at the end of Via Constantinopoli before reaching Piazza della Vittoria. The huge wall to the left is a common urban feature in Italy: it bordered the garden of Villa d'Alessandro, a private mansion. (NARA via Digital History Archive)

the Canadians would make a dash to Piazza Municipale leaving the Germans behind, and clear the area afterwards. This enabled a swift advance to a rubble obstacle barring the way to Piazza Municipale, from which the Germans started firing on the tanks and the infantry. Unable to move forward, the LER took up positions in the houses on both sides of Corso Vittorio Emanuele, clearing them and discovering that the pile of rubble had been mined.

B Company, using the previous tactics, made a steady advance along Corso Garibaldi, which ended at the pile of rubble blocking access to Piazza Municipale. All three companies spent the rest of the day clearing the houses and securing their foothold in the old town. The SHC's D Company advanced along Via Rapino facing strong German opposition, the rest of the battalion sheltering at the Santa Maria church under German mortar fire. The battalion moved to Piazza della Vittoria later that same day.

The 23rd of December was a decisive day. While the LER moved into Piazza Municipale, defended by one anti-tank gun and at least five machine-gun nests, the SHC was fully committed on the western flank to isolate the area. In the meantime, the anti-tank guns of CDN 90th Battery started pounding the houses on the eastern side of Ortona, above the railway station.

'MOUSEHOLING' IN ORTONA, 23 DECEMBER 1943 (PP. 82–83)

By 23 December, after four days of heavy fighting, the men of the LER (known as the 'Eddies') and the SHC, supported by the tanks of the TRR, were now entering the old part of Ortona, at the heart of the town. As they approached the 'killing zone' set by the Fallschirmjäger, the fighting became harder and the risks increased. Clearing the houses, the Canadians discovered that the Germans had booby-trapped the entrances (and the interiors too) to the buildings. The men of D and A companies of the LER soon developed their tactics. Using plastic explosives, they would make a hole in the wall dividing two houses, and use it to enter and clean out the building while the Germans were still stunned by the explosion. This technique was known as 'mouseholing'. As well as plastic explosives, the PIAT anti-tank gun was also used (**1**), as seen here carried by the gunner.

On 23 December, the TRR added the 3rd Troop from A Squadron and 4th Troop from C Squadron to support the men of D and A companies advancing along the central Corso Vittorio Emanuele (with B Company moving along Corso Garibaldi) approaching the Piazza Municipale. Ortona's roads, when not blocked by rubble obstacles, were covered in debris (**2**). The TRR's Sherman Mk Vs from A and C squadrons (**3**) provided essential support to the infantry (**4**), which was exposed to enemy fire whenever approaching a road junction or a square (piazza). *Challenger*, the Sherman from C Squadron seen here, carries the usual amount of stowage and sports the formation sign (a yellow circle for C Squadron, **5**). It was not uncommon for tanks to have their serial number repeated twice on the hull side (**6**).

Both battalions having been reinforced by another tank troop from A and C squadrons, TRR, the SHC were directed to protect the LER's left flank with B Company advancing along the rubble-free road four streets away from Corso Vittorio Emanuele. The rest of the SHC would move with A Company advancing two streets away facing similar conditions, and D Company continuing to advance along Via Rapino.

The engineers and the anti-tank guns, firing to clear the rubble obstacle, opened the way to Piazza Municipale for D Company, LER, which was immediately engaged by three German machine guns located in a building on the left side of the square. Private Rattray, and two others, entered the building, and while the latter dealt with the Germans on the ground floor, Rattray was able to capture the three machine guns and their crews. A Company then entered the square followed by the Shermans of 4th Troop, which were halted by the hidden German anti-tank gun. A methodical, slow and exhausting clearing of all the houses in the square began, a process of intense violence.

The crew of a Canadian 3in. mortar firing in Ortona. Apart from tanks providing direct fire support, anti-tank guns were used in the town where no artillery support was possible. In its absence, heavy mortars provided the necessary firepower. (NARA via Digital History Archive)

The usual tactic for clearing a building was to enter via the front door and clear it room by room. Soon, the Canadians discovered that the Germans had predicted this, and booby-trapped doors and pieces of furniture. Also, they defended the upper floors, making the clearing process slow and dangerous. An ingenious way to solve this problem was found, dubbed 'mouseholing'. An explosive charge was placed on a wall, which collapsed after the explosion. The Germans in the nearby house would be stunned, and easily overcome by the Canadians. PIATs were also used later in place of explosives.

As A and D companies cleared the square in the morning, with the Shermans eventually silencing the anti-tank gun at 1100hrs, B Company advanced along Corso Umberto I and reached its northern end. At the end of the day, as the tanks withdrew to refuel and to rest their crews, the infantry supported by the anti-tank guns consolidated their positions. The SHC's B Company, attached, began moving along the parallel road; facing challenging German defences, it took two hours to advance 50m. As A Company advanced two roads away, and with D Company moving along Via Rapino before turning north, at 1800hrs the SHC was able to establish defensive positions in the narrow streets while the Germans, in the darkness, infiltrated their lines and continued to destroy buildings.

Lance-Corporal E.A. Harris, from the LER, firing at a German position in Ortona. The successful Canadian handling of the battle was partly due to previous training in urban warfare. (Public domain)

On 24 December, General Heidrich, 1.Fallschirmjäger-Division's commander, deployed his only available reserve – II./FJR 4 – in Ortona to support the now depleted II./FJR 3. This, and the fact that the Canadians entered the 'killing zones', intensified the ferocity of the fighting inside the town. The arrival of replacements proved troublesome for the Canadian commanders, who found their men to be undertrained and lacking experience. Nevertheless, this did not halt their attacking. That same day, as A Squadron, TRR replaced C Squadron, the LER moved from the northern and eastern exits of Piazza Municipale towards the town hall, the central Piazza Plebiscito and Corso Umberto I, linking up with B Company.

The fresh Fallschirmjäger prevented any rapid advance of the LER companies, with buildings having to be taken for a second time after the Germans seized them by infiltrating the Canadian lines. By the end of the day, the LER had managed to reach the southern end of Piazza Plebiscito and of Corso Umberto I, the gateway to the heart of the German defence: the San Tommaso cathedral and the nearby market square. In the meantime, the SHC continued its advance, aiming at Piazza San Francesco, the Santa Maria delle Grazie church at its centre and the large school building across the street to the east.

A Company, SHC was the first to reach the entrance to the square, securing two buildings in front of the church. Since the company commander, Captain June Thomas, spotted a dead horse in front of the church, the square would be known as 'Dead Horse Square'. Facing the Fallschirmjäger defending the church and the school, A Company, supported by tanks, was able to seize the

school building for the loss of just a single casualty. The reason behind the easy seizure of the building was revealed just after dark when a delayed charge exploded, destroying most of it and killing five. This was not the only German move; protected by a machine gun in the bell tower, the Fallschirmjäger swarmed into the square to eject the Canadians from it. The first, large-scale German counter-attack was beaten off, the machine gun being silenced by a Sherman, and the men of the SHC returned to 'mouseholing' their way into the buildings. This proved particularly difficult in the church, where the Germans strongly defended the pulpit zone.

At the end of 24 December, the SHC's D Company had reached the western portion of 'Dead Horse Square', A Company held the southern end and B Company held its south-eastern sector. The buildings all around the square were playing host to both Canadian and German soldiers.

The arrival of German reinforcements and the intensity of the fighting explains why the pace of the Canadian advance had slowed. On Christmas Day, as a dinner was held at Santa Maria di Constantinopoli, both the LER and SHC made little progress. The plan was to split the German defences and prevent infiltration, and for that reason the LER was to advance with D Company moving north of Piazza Plebiscito to Via Tripoli, with the aim of linking up with the SHC advancing from 'Dead Horse Square' along Via Monte Maiella. A Company was to turn and advance towards the San Tommaso cathedral, while B Company continued its advance along Corso Umberto I.

A Canadian soldier inspecting a German machine-gun nest in the Ortona area; the bench in the background clearly suggests an urban setting, most likely placing this in Ortona's southern outskirts. (Keystone/Getty Images)

A Canadian gunner from the LER Anti-Tank Battery of the CDN 1st Infantry Division fires a 6-pdr QF anti-tank gun against positions held by troops of 1.Fallschirmjäger-Division in Ortona on 21 December 1943. (Photo by Terry F. Rowe/Keystone/Hulton Archive/Getty Images)

The main hurdle was the large pile of rubble at the southern end of Piazza Plebiscito, which prevented tank movement and was under sniper, machine-gun and mortar fire. Still, a Sherman was able to approach the obstacle and fire on the Germans, exposing only its turret. A house which hosted a nest of Fallschirmjäger was destroyed by a 6-pdr gun, manhandled into position up the pile of rubble by Bombardier Doucette and his crew. 'Mouseholing' into the southern end of Piazza Plebiscito was then begun by D Company, which eventually was forced to withdraw due to German resistance.

A Company only managed to reach the south-west corner of Piazza San Tommaso before German resistance halted its advance, and B Company hardly advanced at all while guns and tanks pounded the buildings on Corso Umberto I, the eastern entrance of the railway tunnel and the empty castle. Exhaustion, and renewed German efforts, saw the SHC still fighting in 'Dead Horse Square', the only progress being made by 1st Troop, C Squadron, TRR, which advanced along Via Cavour from Piazza Municipale to reach the square. Once there, the tanks fired relentlessly on the church, until it collapsed. Following a radio broadcast, Ortona became known as 'Little Stalingrad', which made the Germans even more determined to hold it.

On 26 December, the Canadian attack reached its zenith. After clearing the rubble obstacle blocking the way to Piazza Plebiscito, D Company, LER (down to 18 men) cleared the square supported by tanks, and soon faced two German anti-tank guns. After destroying one and damaging the

other, the Germans were driven away from most of the square by another tank troop just as A Company, advancing along the northern end of Corso Vittorio Emanuele, faced a strong German position in the rubble created by the destruction of the cathedral. B Company approached from the south, along Corso Umberto I.

What turned the tide was the discovery of the tunnel network used by the Germans, which the Canadian engineers destroyed at once. By the end of the day, the LER controlled most of Piazza Plebiscito and the southern entrance to Piazza San Tommaso. At 'Dead Horse Square' the SHC faced yet another German counter-attack, the Fallschirmjäger infiltrating their positions and capturing two sections from C Company. The prompt intervention of C Squadron's 2nd Troop, TRR saved the situation, as the Shermans pounded every building in the square for more than two hours. Eventually, the SHC men were released, and the remaining Fallschirmjäger withdrew.

From 1400hrs, the SHC was on the move, A Company heading up Via Cavour, C Company linking up with B Company before advancing along Via Monte Maiella and D Company mopping up the square. The former halted at the end of the day at the south-west corner of Piazza Municipale, the latter 100m before reaching Via Roma. During the night, the Germans

Three Fallschirmjäger, one of whom is severely wounded, surrender to the men of C Company, SHC at the end of Via Constantinopoli, Ortona. The actual number of German soldiers taken prisoner at Ortona remains unclear. (Hulton Archive/Getty Images)

shelled the Canadian positions and infiltrated their lines, but the battle was nearing its end.

Facing the threat of Orsogna being cut off and having no reserves, at 1100hrs General Lemelsen ordered the withdrawal from the town. Prior to this, the fighting continued with a platoon from A Company, LER being wiped out when the building they had entered was blown up. As the LER struggled to enter Piazza San Tommaso, the SHC's B and C companies advanced to the entrance to Via Roma and Via Tripoli, where they joined D Company, LER, which had cleared Piazza Plebiscito. A and B companies, LER seized key buildings, giving them a clear line of fire across the entire Piazza San Tommaso. The Canadians had now reached the northern limits of Ortona.

At 1540hrs, a dozen German fighter-bombers swept over the town dropping bombs. Fearing a German counter-attack, Brigadier Hoffmeister directed the PPCLI to prepare for the final assault into Ortona. At 2230hrs, the Fallschirmjäger silently withdrew from the town, leaving the Canadians to discover that the battle was over the next morning. It had cost the LER 63 killed and 109 wounded, with the SHC losing 41 killed and 62 wounded. The TRR had lost four killed and 20 wounded, three Shermans being total write-offs. The losses incurred by 1.Fallschirmjäger-Division from 20 to 28 December in and around Ortona were 68 killed, 159 wounded and 205 missing; it remains impossible to say how many of these were in the fighting for the town.

AFTERMATH

On 30 December, General Montgomery relinquished command of BR Eighth Army to General Oliver Leese and left for Britain. This effectively marked the end of the offensive on the Adriatic flank, and the failure of Alexander's two-pronged attack plan on Rome.

US Fifth Army continued its advance from San Pietro Infine, slowly and steadily. While BR X Corps patrolled the Garigliano, US II Corps attacked again on 3 January 1944, three days later seizing the key features of Mount Majo and San Vittore, Mount Porchia falling on the 9th. The Germans withdrew, leaving in their hands only the Mount Trocchio area east of the Garigliano–Rapido River line. This came under attack from 10 January 1944 by US II Corps, which moved against Mount Trocchio on the 15th and seized it the next day. Almost seamlessly, the battle for Cassino began, with the BR X Corps crossing the Garigliano on 17 January and the US 36th Division crossing the Rapido River on 20 January.

Two US infantrymen look towards Monte Cassino and its abbey, where fighting would last from January to May 1944. This was partly because the lessons of the fighting on the Winter Line had not been learned, and Allied commanders insisted on adhering to their original plans. (NARA via Digital History Archive)

The fact that the Winter Line fighting brought to an end Alexander's plan did little to change the determination of Allied commanders to carry out a landing south of Rome. On 8 November 1943, General Alexander chose the Anzio area for the landing, now intended to disrupt the German defences and enable the US Fifth Army to advance on Rome. General Clark accepted the proposal, and a plan (codenamed *Shingle*) was developed. Problems with the availability of landing craft and developments on the Winter Line led both Alexander and Clark on 18 December to consider cancelling *Shingle*.

Following a series of changes at the top levels of Allied command, starting with General Eisenhower being replaced by General Wilson, the *Shingle* plan was revived. A decisive step came on 19 December, and again on the 23rd, when the British Prime Minister Winston Churchill pressed for results in Italy. Given the situation at the front, the landing seemed the only chance of achieving them. Having secured the necessary landing craft, on 25 December Alexander informed Clark that *Shingle* could be carried out as planned. Less than a month later, the battle for Cassino – and a new phase of the Italian campaign – began.

A 20mm Flak 38 gun on the Italian front in early 1944. As shown on the shield, this particular weapon has shot down five enemy aircraft. Given their marked inferiority in the air, anti-aircraft guns provided German forces with their principal means of protection against Allied air attacks. (Narodowe Archiwum Cyfrowe)

THE BATTLEFIELDS TODAY

After the war, a new town of San Pietro Infine was built close to the ruins of the old one, which were partly restored but only to be used as a set for war movies, or as a tourist attraction. In 2008 a dedicated *Parco della Memoria* (Remembrance Park) was built in an old mill at San Pietro, recreating with images and sound life in the town and its experiences of war. In spite of the unavoidable changes due to time and human efforts, a visit to San Pietro Infine remains likely to evoke the drama of the battle fought in December 1943.

Orsogna was rebuilt and was developed after the war, but its main features are still very noticeable. Apart from the geographical ones, one ought to remark how the town centre still matches the town's former architectural style. Given that Orsogna lies only a brief car journey away from Ortona (and be careful not to mix the two up), visiting both is recommended.

Ortona was rebuilt after the war and, like Orsogna, it expanded as well, becoming a much bigger town than it used to be. Again, most of the city centre matches the town's old identity, in some cases with walls still bearing warnings and notices for the soldiers written in 1944. More importantly, Ortona has a small but extremely well maintained, and precious, museum of the battle created by the municipality in 2002. Albeit small, it is indeed worth visiting. The exhibits include, amongst others, a large diorama showing the battle fought in the old town.

A modern photo of Orsogna and its surrounding countryside, Abruzzo, Italy. (DeAgostini/Getty Images)

FURTHER READING

After the Battle issue No. 18 (*The Battle for San Pietro*), No. 183 (*The Battle of Ortona*), No. 192 (*The Battle for Orsogna*)

Blumenson, Martin, *Salerno to Cassino* (Washington, DC: Center of Military History US Army, 1993)

Bowlby, Alex, *Countdown to Cassino: The Battle of Mignano Gap, 1943* (New York, NY: Sarpedon, 1995)

Brown, Shaun R.G., '"The Rock of Accomplishment": The Loyal Edmonton Regiment at Ortona', *Canadian Military History*, 2:2 (1993)

Center of Military History US Army, *Fifth Army at the Winter Line (15 November 1943–15 January 1944)* (Washington, DC: Center of Military History US Army, 1990)

Daskevich, Col. Anthony F. II, 'Insights into Modularity: the 753rd Tank Battalion in World War II' (US Army War College report, 2008)

Donth, Rudolf, *Die Geschichte der Fallschirmjäger Regiment 4, 1942–1945* (Schongau, 1991)

Forsythe, Col. John D., *Fifth Army History, 16 November 1943–15 January 1944*, Vol. III: *The Winter Line* (Florence, n.d.)

Geroux, Jason, 'The Urban Battle of Ortona', MA Thesis, University of New Brunswick (2020)

Golla, Karl-Heinz, *Zwischen Reggio und Cassino: Das Kriegsgeschehen in Italien im zweiten Halbjahr 1943* (Bonn: Bernard & Graefe, 2004)

Greenfield, Kent Roberts (ed.), *Command Decisions* (Washington, DC: USGPO, 1960)

Grigg, John, *1943. The Victory that Never Was* (London: Faber and Faber, 2013)

Malatesta, Saverio, *Orsogna 1943: La battaglia per la linea Gustav nella 'Cassino dell'Adriatico'* (Ortona: Menabò, 2016)

Molony, Brigadier C.J.C., *The Mediterranean and the Middle East*, Vol. V: *The Campaign in Sicily 1943 and the Campaign in Italy, 3rd September 1943 to 31st March 1944* (London: HMSO, 1973)

Nicholson, Lt.Col. G.W.L., *The Canadians in Italy 1943–1945* (Ottawa: Queen's Printer, 1956)

Patricelli, Marco, *La Stalingrado d'Italia: Ortona 1943, una battaglia dimenticata* (Turin: UTET, 2002)

Phillips, N.C., *Italy*, Vol. I: *The Sangro to Cassino* (Wellington: War History Branch, 1957)

Plowman, Jeffrey, *Orsogna: New Zealand's First Italian Battle* (Christchurch: Wilsonscott, 2010)

Pugsley, Christopher, *A Bloody Road Home: World War Two and New Zealand's Heroic Second Division* (Auckland: Penguin, 2014)

Ronchetti, Gabriele and Ferrara, Maria Angela, *La linea Gustav: I luoghi delle battaglie da Ortona a Cassino* (Fidenza: Mattioli 1885, 2014)

Wagner, Robert L., *The Texas Army: A History of the 36th Division in the Italian Campaign* (Austin, TX: Robert L. Wagner, 1972)

Walker, Fred L., *From Texas to Rome: Fighting World War II and the Italian Campaign with the 36th Infantry Division* (Austin, TX: Robert L. Wagner, 1972)

Zuehlke, Mark, *Ortona: Canada's Epic World War II Battle* (Vancouver: Douglas & McIntyre, 1999)

Zuehlke, Mark, *Ortona: Street Fight* (Victoria: Orca, 2011)

INDEX

Figures in **bold** refer to illustrations.